WHITE SLAVES

A History of the Enslavement of White people in Early America and the world.

Sir Patrick Bijou

Copyright © 2023 Sir Patrick Bijou

BIJOUEBOOKS
All Rights Reserved.

This work is subject to copyright. All rights are solely and exclusively licensed by the Publisher, whether the whole or part of the material is concerned, specially the rights of translation, reprinting, reuse of illustrations, recitation, broadcasting, reproduction on microfilms or in any other physical way, and transmission or information storage and retrieval, electronic adaptation, computer software, or by similar or dissimilar methodology now known or hereafter developed.

The use of general descriptive names, registered names, trademarks, service marks, etc. in this publication does not imply, even in the absence of a specific statement, that such names are exempt from the relevant protective laws and regulations and therefore free for general use.

The publisher, the authors and the editors are safe to assume that the advice and information in this book are believed to be true and accurate at the date of publication. Neither the publisher nor the authors or the editors give a warranty, expressed or implied, with respect to the material contained herein or for any errors or omissions that may have been made. The publisher remains neutral with regard to jurisdictional claims in published maps and institutional affiliations.

Cover design copyright © 2023 by Sir Patrick Bijou
BIJOUEBOOKS
All Rights Reserved.

ABOUT THE AUTHOR

Sir Patrick Bijou lives and writes from the United Kingdom and is the author of several books on finance and fiction. He is known for his extraordinary skills in settling and negotiating peace settlements and international law and is a prodigious legal and political adviser. His diverse writing ability has been influenced by many experiences, making him the success he is today.

He has written many books and articles about the liberation of people, highlighting the issues of those whom the literary world of creative writing has not enlightened. His expedition into content writing has made him a remarkable and inspired author and professional communicator.

He has written over 45 non-fictional and fictional books spanning different genres, including finance, fiction, and self-development. Sir Patrick was born in South America on the first day of December

1958 to an Amerindian mother (late Esther) and a mixed-race father of Amerindian and African descent (late Eric). His grandmother was an African who originated from the city that is now Sekondi-Takoradi in Ghana, West Africa. Her mother was an enslaved African in the proclamation of labour to British Guiana, now Guyana, to work and serve on the sugar plantations that today brand Guyana famous for its Demerara sugar.

His Excellency was extremely fond of his African grandmother and his African roots. Sadly, he had only spent a short time with her and was taken away to England by his father. His Excellency was determined to explore his roots and visited the village where his grandmother was born and spent time in the region. He recounts the memory of a sense of belonging when visiting his ancestors' town and feeling an overwhelming spiritual sense of serenity, beauty and peace. So intense was the feeling of calm that it left an indelible and lasting feeling of his profound connection to Africa and its people.

Sir Patrick excelled in becoming a highly educated and intellectual academic. Aside from being a notable investment banker, he is also a Fund Manager, professional communicator, best-selling author, and philanthropist. His intelligence and educational strides are evident in his role in multi-national organisations and financial institutions. He was knighted under the Directory of the Sovereignty of the Knights of Malta for his services to banking and charity.

His Excellency is a Global Ambassador for the International Rights and Welfare Association (IRAWA) and Ambassador of the Royal Diplomatic Club. In May 2021, he was appointed Ambassador by

The Academy of Universal Global Peace U.S.A. as a member of the governing board/trustees and awarded The Human Excellency Award.

He is the President of International Banking Relations of the Commonwealth Entrepreneurs Club and Ambassador for the UNWPA (United Nations World Peace Association).

Finding his Books.
To find out more about Sir Patrick, visit his website.
www.sirpatrickbijou.com
www.bijouebook.com

Table of Contents

Introduction 1

White Slavery in Ancient & Medieval Europe 3

Arabs and the Traffic in White Slaves 5

Viking Slavers 8

White Slavery in Early America 10

A Holocaust Against The White Poor 15

The Political Economy of the Industrial Revolution 21

The Factory System 29

Human Brooms 38

Breaking the Chains of Illusion 47

Poor Whites and the Southern Confederacy 51

Whites Were the First Slaves in America 58

Irish Slaves 69

Protestant Slaves 71

Legal Basis and Definitions 72

White Political Prisoners Sold into Slavery 78

Slave Hunting in Britain 81

White Children in Chains 85

White Losses in the Middle Passage Higher than that of Blacks 92

White Slaves Treated Worse than Blacks 99

Indentures: An Organized Racket 101

Enslavement of the White Family	109
When Hell was in Session	112
The Fugitive Slave Law: Escaping Whites Hunted and Tortured	115
White Slaves in the American Revolution	124
White Slave Rebellions	127
Torture and Murder of White Slaves	135
Crackers, Redlegs, Rednecks and Hillbillies	140
The Death of Two "Human Brooms"	147
A Childhood in the Factory	149
Alabama Sharecropper — 1936	151
End Notes	152
Glossary of Terms	165
Bibliography	171

Introduction

"They were of two sorts, first such as were brought over by masters of ships to be sold as servants. Such as we call them my dear,' says she, 'but they are more properly called slaves." — Daniel Defoe, *Moll Flanders*

This is a history of White people that has never been told in any coherent form, largely because most modern historians have, for reasons of politics or psychology, refused to recognize White slaves in early America as just that.

Today, not a tear is shed for the sufferings of millions of white slaves. 200 years of White slavery in America have been almost completely obliterated from the collective memory of the American people.

Who wants to be reminded that half—perhaps as many as thirds—of the original American colonists came here, not of their own free will, but kidnapped, shanghaied, impressed, duped, beguiled, and yes, in chains?... we tend to gloss over it... we'd prefer to forget the whole sorry chapter..." (Elaine Kendall, *Los Angeles Times,* Sept. 1, 1985).

A correct understanding of the authentic history of the enslavement of Whites in America could have profound consequences for the future of the races: "We cannot be sure that the position of the earliest Africans differed markedly from that of the white indentured servants. The debate has considerable significance for the interpretation of race relations in American history" (Eugene D. Genovese, *Roll, Jordan Roll: The World the Slaves Made,* p. 31).

Most of the books on White labor in early America are titled with words like "White indentured servitude," White "bondservants," White "servants" etc. It is interesting that White people who were bound to a condition of what became in many cases permanent chattel slavery unto death, are not referred to as slaves by Establishment academics.

With the massive concentration of educational and media resources on the negro experience of slavery the unspoken assumption has been that only Blacks have been enslaved to any degree or magnitude worthy of study or memorial. The historical record reveals that this is not the case, however. White people have been sold as slaves for centuries.

White Slavery in Ancient & Medieval Europe

Among the ancient Greeks, despite their tradition of democracy, the enslavement of fellow Whites— even fellow Greeks—was the order of the day. Aristotle considered White slaves as things. The Romans also had no compunctions against enslaving Whites who they too termed "a thing" *(res)*. In his agricultural writings, the first century B.C. Roman philosopher Varro labeled White slaves as nothing more than "tools that happened to have voices" *(instrumenti vocale)*. Cato the Elder, discoursing on plantation management, proposed that White slaves when old or ill should be discarded along with worn-out farm implements.

Julius Caesar enslaved as many as one million Whites from Gaul, some of whom were sold to the slave dealers who followed his victorious legions (William D. Phillips, Jr., *Slavery from Roman Times to the Early Transatlantic Trade*, p.18).

In A.D. 319 the "Christian" emperor of Rome, Constantine, ruled that if an owner whipped his White slave to death "he should not stand in any criminal accusation if the slave dies; and all statutes of limitations and legal interpretations are hereby set aside."

The Romans enslaved thousands of the early White inhabitants of Great Britain who were known as "Angles," from which we derive the term "Anglo-Saxon" as a description of the

English race. In the sixth century Pope Gregory the First witnessed blond-haired, blue-eyed English boys awaiting sale in a slave market in Rome. Inquiring of their origin, the Pope was told they were Angles. Gregory replied, "Non Angli, sed Angeli" ("Not Angles, but Angels").

When the Franks conquered the Visigoths in southern Gaul huge numbers of Whites entered the slave markets. "After Charlemagne's conquest of Saxony, during which many pagan Saxons were enslaved, he set up a network of parish churches. To provide for the maintenance of the priest and the church, those living in the parish were to donate a house and land as well as a male and female (Saxon) slave to the church for every 120 people in the parish" (William Phillips. p. 52).

Arabs and the Traffic in White Slaves

The trade in White slaves was one of the few sources of foreign exchange for western European powers in a period when the East produced the goods that Europeans could not procure elsewhere. The sale of White slaves to Asia and Africa was one of the few sources of gold for European treasuries.

From the eighth to the eleventh century France was a major transfer point for White slaves to the Muslim world, with Rouen being the center for the selling of Irish and Flemish slaves.

"At the same time that France was a transfer point for slaves to the Muslim world, Italy was occupying much the same position... Venetians (were)... selling slaves and timber across the Mediterranean. The slaves were usually Slavs brought across the Alps... The Venetians were the earliest successful Italian sea traders and because profits on (slave) trade with the Muslims were lucrative, they resisted efforts to stop them. In return for their exports of timber, iron and (White) slaves, they brought in oriental luxury products, mainly fine cloths..." (William Phillips, pp. 62-63).

The stereotype from Establishment consensus history is of the Muslim slaver herding chained Blacks through the desert. In fact, for seven hundred years, until the fall of Muslim Spain, those being herded were first and foremost overwhelmingly White:

"Before the tenth century the Muslims generally bought Christian Europeans as slaves... By the tenth century, Slavs became the most numerous imported group... during the late Middle Ages, until the fall of Granada in the late fifteenth century, most slaves of the... Muslims were Christians from the northern kingdoms..." (William Phillips, p. 69).

"In the vast lands of the eastern European steppes from the eighth to the twelfth century, there was a well-developed slaving network... Slavs and Finns, called *saqaliba* (slaves) indiscriminately by the Muslims, entered the Muslim world by these Caspian and Black sea routes." (William Phillips, pp. 63-64).

The fate of the hundreds of thousands of White slaves sold to the Arabs was described in one Spanish text as *"atrocissima et ferocissima"* (most atrocious and harsh). The men were worked to death as galley slaves. The women, girls and boys were used as prostitutes.

White males had their genitals mutilated in castration attempts—bloody procedures of incredible brutality which most of the White men who were forced to submit did not survive, judging from the high prices White eunuchs commanded throughout the Middle Eastern slave markets.

Escape from North Africa and the Middle East was almost impossible and those White slaves who were caught trying to flee were punished by having their noses and ears cut off, or worse.

Early Muslim texts provide insights into the extent to which the Arabs identified Europeans with slavery, classified White slaves as animals and even produced learned racist disquisitions on the supposed merits of emasculated East European slaves. In his ninth century treatise on beasts, *The Book of Animals,* the Muslim scholar Jahiz writes:

"Another change which overcomes the eunuch: of two slaves of Slavic race, who are... twins, one castrated and the other not, the eunuch becomes more disposed toward service, wiser, more able, and apt for various problems of manual labor... All these qualities you find only in the castrated one. On the other hand, his brother continues to have the same native torpor, the same lack of natural talent, the same imbecility common to slaves, and incapacity for learning a foreign language." (Charles Verlinden, *The Slave in Medieval Europe,* vol. 1, p. 213).

Whites were also enslaved in Russia and I do not refer here to serfdom which was a later development: "Knowledge of the existence of slavery in early modern Russia is not widespread. Many people know of the existence of serfdom, and confuse the two" (Richard Hellie, *Slavery in Russia, 1450-1725,* p. xvii).

The White Russian Muscovites were enslaved both by northern European raiders as well as massive slave-catching operations launched by the Mongols and the Ottoman empire. Russians also enslaved each other to such an extent that in 1571 an official Slave Chancellery was established which formally codified White slavery as a Russian institution. (Hellie, p. 118).

Viking Slavers

In the ninth century the Vikings sold tens of thousands of Whites to the Arabs of Spain. According to Michael Wood's book In Search of the Dark Ages:

"An Arab traveler of the time who came to Spain remarked on the great numbers of European slaves in harems and in the militia. The palace of the Emir of Cordoba in particular had many White girls... Of these unfortunate people the Vikings were undoubtedly a major source of supply... The Arabs in Spain saw the long-term potential of this trade, and as early as the 840s sent a diplomatic mission to Scandinavia to put it on an organized basis."

"The most westerly component of the early medieval slave trade in Europe was the British Isles. In the eleventh century the Vikings were active slave traders in Ireland... From Ireland the Vikings took the slaves to be sold in Muslim Spain and Scandinavia, and even to be transported into Russia; some may have been taken as far as Constantinople and the Muslim Middle East..." (William Phillips, p. 63).

"The Norwegian slave trader was an important enough figure to appear in the 12th century tale of Tristan... Icelandic literature also provides numerous references to raiding in Ireland as a source for slaves...

"Norwegian Vikings made slave raids not only against the Irish and Scots (who are often called Irish in Norse sources) but also against Norse settlers in Ireland or the Scottish Isles or even in

Norway itself... Slave trading was a major commercial activity of the Viking Age... (Ruth Mazo Karras, Slavery and Society in Medieval Scandinavia, p. 49). The children of White slaves in Iceland were routinely murdered en masse (Karras, p. 52).

White Slavery in Early America

David Brion Davis writing in the *New York Review of Books,* Oct. 11, 1990, p. 37 states:

"As late as the fourteenth and fifteenth centuries, continuing shipments of white slaves, some of them Christians, flowed from the booming slave markets on the northern Black Sea coast into Italy, Spain, Egypt and the Mediterranean islands... From Barbados to Virginia, colonists.., showed few scruples about reducing their less fortunate countrymen to a status little different from that of chattel slaves... The prevalence and suffering of white slaves, serfs and indentured servants in the early modern period suggests that there was nothing inevitable about limiting plantation slavery to people of African origin."

L. Ruchames in "The Sources of Racial Thought in Colonial America," states that "the slave trade worked in both directions, with white merchandise as well as black." (*Journal of Negro History,* no. 52, pp. 251-273).

In 1659 the English parliament debated the practice of selling British Whites into slavery in the New World. In the debate the Whites were referred to not as "indentured servants" but as "slaves" whose "enslavement" threatened the liberties of all Englishmen. (Thomas Burton, *Parliamentary Diary: 1656-59,* vol. 4, pp. 253-274).

Foster R. Dulles in *Labor in America* quotes an early document describing White children in colonial servitude as "crying and mourning for redemption from their slavery."

Dr. Hilary McD. Beckles of the University of Hull, England, writes regarding White slave labor, "...indenture contracts were alienable... the ownership of which could easily be transferred, like that of any other commodity... as with slaves, ownership changed without their participation in the dialogue concerning transfer." Beckles refers to "indentured servitude" as "White proto-slavery" (*The Americas,* vol. 41, no. 2, p. 21).

In the *Calendar of State Papers, Colonial Series; America and West Indies* of 1701, we read of a protest over the "encouragement to the spiriting away of Englishmen without their consent and selling them for slaves, which hath been a practice very frequent and known by the name of kidnapping." (Emphasis added). In the British West Indies, plantation slavery was instituted as early as 1627. In Barbados by the 1640s there were an estimated 25,000 slaves, of whom 21,700 were White.

("Some Observations on the Island of Barbados," *Calendar of State Papers, Colonial Series,* p. 528). It is worth noting that while White slaves were worked to death in Barbados, there were Caribbean Indians brought from Guiana to help propagate native foodstuffs who were well-treated and received as free persons by the wealthy planters.

Of the fact that the wealth of Barbados was founded on the backs of White slave labor there can be no doubt. White slave laborers from Britain and Ireland were the mainstay of the sugar colony. Until the mid-1640s there were few Blacks in Barbados. George Downing wrote to John Winthrop, the colonial governor of Massachusetts in 1645, that planters who wanted to make a fortune in the British West Indies must procure White slave labor "out of England" if they wanted to succeed. (Elizabeth Donnan, *Documents Illustrative of the History of the Slave Trade to America,* pp. 125-126).

"...white indentured servants were employed and treated, incidentally, exactly like slaves..." (Morley Ayearst, *The British West Indies,* p. 19).

"The many gradations of unfreedom among Whites made it difficult to draw fast lines between any idealized free White worker and a pitied or scorned servile Black worker... in labor-short seventeenth and eighteenth-century America the work of slaves and that of White servants were virtually interchangeable in most areas." (David R. Roediger, *The Wages of Whiteness: Race and the Making of the American Working Class,* p. 25).

In the Massachusetts Court of Assistants, whose records date to 1633, we find a 1638 description of a White man, one Gyles Player, as having been "delivered up for a slave."

The Englishman William Eddis, after observing White slaves in America in the 1770s wrote, "Generally speaking, they groan beneath a worse than Egyptian bondage" (*Letters from America,* London, 1792). Governor Sharpe of the Maryland colony compared the property interest of the planters in their White slaves, with the estate of an English farmer consisting of a "Multitude of Cattle."

The Quock Walker case in Massachusetts in 1 783 which ruled that slavery was contrary to the state Constitution, was applied equally to Blacks and Whites in Massachusetts.

Patrick F. Moran in his *Historical Sketch of the Persecutions Suffered by the Catholics of Ireland,* refers to the transportation of the Irish to the colonies as the "slave-trade" (pp. 343-346).

The disciplinary and revenue laws of early Virginia (circa 1631-1645) did not discriminate Negroes in bondage from

Whites in bondage. (William Hening [editor], *Statutes at Large of Virginia*, vol. I, pp. 174, 198, 200, 243, 306. For records of wills in which "Lands, goods & chattels, cattle, moneys, negroes, English servants, horses, sheep and household stuff" were all sold together see the Lancaster County Records in *Virginia Colonial Abstracts*, Beverly Fleet, editor).

Lay historian Col. A.B. Ellis, writing in the British newspaper *Argosy* (May 6, 1893): "Few, but readers of old colonial State papers and records, are aware that between the years 1649-1690 a lively trade was carried on between England and the plantations, as the colonies were then called, in political prisoners... where they were sold by auction to the colonists for various terms of years, sometimes for life as slaves."

Sir George Sandys' 1618 plan for Virginia referred to bound Whites assigned to the treasurer's office to "belong to said office for ever." The service of Whites bound to Berkeley's Hundred was deemed "perpetual." (Lewis Cecil Gray, *History of Agriculture in the Southern United States to 1860*, vol. I, pp. 316, 318).

Certainly the enslaved Whites themselves recognized their condition with painful clarity. As one White man, named Abram, who was accused of trying to agitate a rebellion stated to his fellows, "Wherefore should wee stay here and be slaves?"

In a statement smuggled out of the New World and published in London, Whites in bondage did not call themselves "indentured servants." In their writing they referred to themselves as "England's slaves" and England's "merchandise." (Marcellus Rivers and Oxenbridge Foyle, *England's Slavery*, 1659).

Eyewitnesses like Pere Labat who visited the West Indian slave plantations of the 17th century which were built and manned by White slaves labeled them "White slaves" and nothing less (*Memoirs of Pere Labat,* 1693-1705, p. 125). Even Blacks referred to the White forced laborers in the colonies as "white slaves." (Colonial Office, Public Records Office, London, 1667, no. 170)

Sot-Weed Factor, or, a Voyage to Maryland, a pamphlet circulated in 1708, articulates the plight of tens of thousands of pathetic young White girls kidnapped from England and enslaved in colonial America, lamenting that:

In better Times e'er to this Land
I was unhappily Trepan'd; Not then a slave...
But things are changed... Kidnap'd and Fool'd..."

The height of academic and media fraud is revealed in the monopolistic trademark status the official controllers of education and mass communications have successfully established between the definition of the word "slave" and the negro, while labeling descriptions of the historic experience of Whites in slavery a fallacy. Yet the very word "slave," which the establishment's consensus school of history pretends cannot legitimately be applied to Whites, is derived from the word Slav. According to the Oxford English Dictionary, the word slave is another name for the White people of eastern Europe, the Slavs. (*Compact Edition of the Oxford English Dictionary,* p. 2,858).

In other words, slave has always been a term for and a definition of a servile condition of *White* people. Yet we are told by the professorcrats that it is not correct to refer to Whites as slaves but only as servants, even though the very root of the word is derived from the historical fact of White slavery.(1)

A Holocaust Against The White Poor

White slavery and bondage in British colonial America cannot be fully understood without also understanding how British Whites came to be dehumanized in their homeland across the sea.

The desperate condition of the poor Whites of Britain was most obvious in the cities. The English slums of the 17th, 18th and 19th centuries were pits of White suffering. London's St. Giles was known locally as "Rat's Castle." A policeman who worked the area used metaphors from the insect world to describe the conditions of the poor Whites there, referring to them as "vermin haunted heaps of rags." Opening the door to a tiny shack the policeman discovered:

"Ten, twenty, thirty—who can count them? Men, women, children, for the most part naked, heaped upon the floor like maggots in a cheese... a spectral rising, unshrouded, from a grave of rags." ("On Duty with Inspector Field," in *Household Words,* June 14, 1851, pp. 265-267).

Herman Melville, in his autobiographical account of his first voyage as a sailor, described the same living death in the English port city of Liverpool in 1839:

"...l generally passed through a narrow street called 'Launcelott's-Hey... once passing through this place... l heard a feeble wail... It seemed the low, hopeless, endless wail of someone forever lost.

"At last I advanced to an opening... to deep tiers of cellars beneath a crumbling old warehouse; and there, some fifteen feet below the walk, crouching in nameless squalor, with her head bowed over, was the figure of what had been a woman.

"Her blue arms folded to her livid bosom two shrunken things like children that leaned toward her, one on each side. At first, I knew not whether they were alive or dead... They were dumb and next to dead with want. How they had crawled into that den, I could not tell; but there they had crawled to die.

"...I tried to lift the woman's head; but feeble as she was, she seemed bent upon holding it down. Observing her arms clasped upon her bosom, and that something seemed hidden under the rags there, a thought crossed my mind which impelled me forcibly to withdraw her hands for a moment when I caught glimpse of a meager little babe, the lower part of its body thrust into an old bonnet.

"Its face was dazzling white, even in its squalor; but the closed eyes looked like balls of indigo. It must have been dead some hours... I stood looking down on them, while my whole soul swelled within me; and I asked myself, what right had any body in the wide world to smile and be glad when sights like this were to be seen?" (Melville, *Redburn: His First Voyage,* Anchor Books edition, pp. 173-178).

"Such is the course of nineteen out of twenty of the fatal cases originating in deficiency of food, as they occur among the destitute poor in our large towns—the first effect of the gradual starvation to which these persons are subjected... It is a strange anomaly to see in wealthy, civilized, Christian England, multitudes of men living in the lowest state of physical degradation and absolutely perishing from neglect... the fact is undeniable, that no inconsiderable portion of our fellow-creatures is living on food and in dwellings scarcely fit for brutes—certainly worse provided for than many of our domestic animals, and that the death of numbers is accelerated or indirectly produced by gradual and protracted starvation..." (Joseph Adshead, *Distress in Manchester: Evidence Tabular and Otherwise of the State of the Laboring Classes in 1840-1842,* pp. 49-50).

Charles Darwin's uncle, factory owner Josiah Wedgewood, owned a business that worked White children of five years of age in a chemical factory permeated with lead oxide, a deadly poison. Wedgewood acknowledged that the lead made the children "very subject to disease" but worked them anyway.

The English writer Frances Trollope estimated that at least 200,000 English children were "snatched away" to factories, "...taken and lodged amid stench, and stunning, terrifying tumult; driven to and fro until their little limbs bend under them... the repose of a moment to be purchased only by yielding their tender bodies to the fist, the heel or the strap of the overlooker (overseer)." (Marcus Cunliffe, *Chattel Slavery and Wage Slavery,* p. 73).

In 1723 the Waltham Act was passed which classified more than 200 minor offenses such as stealing a rabbit from an aristocrat or breaking up his fishpond, a crime punishable by hanging. Starving youths, fourteen years old, were strung-up on Tyburn gallows for stealing as little as one sheep. When their bodies were cut down their parents had to fight over, them with agents of the Royal College of Physicians who had been empowered by the courts to use their remains for laboratory dissection.

The English historian William Cobbet stated in 1836, "The starving agricultural laborers of southern England are worse off than American negroes." When in 1 834 English farm workers in Dorset tried to form a union in order to "preserve ourselves, our wives and our children from starvation" they were shipped into slavery in Australia for this "crime." The situation of White factory workers was no better. Robert Owen declared in 1840, "The working classes of Great Britain are in a worse condition than any slaves in any country, in any period of the world's history."

In 19th century England tens of thousands of White children were employed as slave laborers in British coal mines. Little White boys, seven years old, were harnessed like donkeys to coal carts and ordered to drag them through mine shafts. In 1843, White children aged four were working in the coal pits. In old English cemeteries can be seen epitaphs on grave stones like one which reads, "William Smith, aged eight years, Miner, died Jan. 3, 1841."

The root of of the holocaust against the White yeomanry of Britain lies in the history of the land swindles perpetrated against them in the late 12th and early 13th centuries.

As the lords obtained their rights against the king as formalized in the Magna Carta, they used them to expropriate the land rights of the yeoman by means of the writ of novel disseisin and what historian Rodney Hilton describes as other "lawyer's traps." Ownership was transferred to the lords. The people were allowed to remain on their ancestral lands with something akin to a sharecropper's status.

By the 17th century even this tenancy was being eroded by the introduction of the enclosure laws, which fenced off land heretofore farmed in common by the people, as the landlords began to enforce their "property rights." The net effect of enclosure, though it was at first slow in coming, was the eviction of the people from the land, a process begun toward the end of Elizabeth's reign, necessitating the first "poor relief" law for able-bodied, unemployed persons, known as "the 43rd Elizabeth," (after the year of her reign in which it had been enacted, 1601).

This act transformed the old laws concerning community self-help based on voluntary, local almsgiving, to a general tax or "rate-paying," administered through the Church of England for distribution in local parishes.

As noble as the intent of the law may seem, it was little more than a token measure, intended not to halt the flood of misery generated by the dispossession of the British yeomen, but rather to placate the consciences of those who could see all too well the emergence of a new pattern of starvation and poverty, previously known in Britain mainly in times of war or pestilence.

The introduction of the 43rd Elizabeth marked the beginning of a holocaust against the poor of Britain justified by jurists and aristocrats and operated in the absence of the revolution in land reform which would have returned the farms to the people and effected the only genuine remedy for the poverty beginning to grip the working class.

To alleviate the symptoms of the land dispossession, four systems of bondage would evolve: 1. Poor relief. 2. White slavery in the colonies. 3. The workhouse. 4. The factory system. They would all develop their special horrors, each justified by pointing to the evils intrinsic in the previous scheme to "help the poor."

"Poor relief" institutionalized the new stigma of "pauperism" and "parasitism" which the ruling class attached to the impoverished condition of the dispossessed yeomanry, as homelessness and starvation increased.

"It was laid down that all recipients of poor relief should be compelled to wear the letter 'P' on their sleeves, and that they should be whipped if they neglected or refused to do so. The 'P' stood for a word which had already acquired its lasting stigma:

pauper." (Brian Inglis, *Poverty and the Industrial Revolution*, p.17).

The next phase of "relief" for indigent British Whites was their enslavement in the American colonies, which was made acceptable on the basis of the pauperism created by the enclosure laws and the dehumanization of the British poor as a lower order of man (when their humanity was conceded at all). Enslavement on the colonial plantations of America became a "mercy" because it transported Whites of "mean estate" out of the wretched streets and hovels of Britain by means of courts of assize and press gangs.

The Political Economy of the Industrial Revolution

Enslavement overseas would not prove sufficient for the disposal of all of Britain's "surplus" poor, however. The workhouse system, instituted by such High Church Tories as Sir Humphrey Mackworth, flattered itself with the claim that the poor people of Britain were generally in the fix that they were, due to their own "folly" and lack of virtue, and that "habits of thrift and industry" could be instilled by imprisoning them in fortress-like buildings, thereby removing them from the perils of the press-gangs, the assize courts and the street, where the propertied classes would have had to endure the spectacle of their starvation.

The public expenditure connected with the construction and operation of the workhouse system was a source of self-congratulation for the aristocracy. Now the White poor could starve slowly in privacy instead of publicly on the street; with a sop to the conscience in the expectation that some might survive and learn "generosity toward their betters" and "virtuous habits" in the bargain.

In the year 1765, twenty-three indigent children were placed in the care of the St. Clement Danes' workhouse. By January of the following year two had been discharged and eighteen were dead. In the same time-period, of seventy-eight children placed in the care of the workhouse at Holborn, sixty-four were dead. Of eighteen children who entered St. George's Middlesex workhouse, sixteen departed in a coffin. In the workhouse of the combined parishes of St. Giles in the Fields and St. George's Bloomsbury, the mortality rate for English children was 90%, moving one contemporary observer to opine that placing children in the workhouse, "is but a small remove from slaughter, *for the child must die.*" One is reminded of the remark of the English legal scholar William Blackstone, "It is much easier to extirpate than to amend mankind."

As the workhouse was revealed to be a "mansion of putridity," a "humane reform along scientific lines" was called for and into the breach stepped the political economist Jeremy Bentham. Bentham's philosophy viewed the workhouse, when properly implemented according to the latest principles in "pauper administration" and the "panopticon principle of construction," as the "scientific" management of poor Whites.

Bentham's supposedly humane, model "pantopticon workhouse" was even more tomb-like and regimented than its predecessors and amounted to the creation of a prison warehouse for the storage of that vexatious species of humanity, the White "pauper."[1]

An expose' of political economy appears in Charles Dickens' *Oliver Twist* in his characterization of the Bentham and Ricardo "philosophers" on the board of supervisors of a workhouse:

"The members of this board were very sage, deep, philosophical men, and when they came to turn their attention to the workhouse, they found out at once, what ordinary folks would

---

[1] Bentham had his elderly butler hanged for stealing two silver spoons. (John Vincent, "Hanging: A Weapon of Class War," *Sunday Telegraph,* Nov. 24, 1991).

never have discovered—that poor people liked it! It was a regular place of public entertainment for the poorer classes... a brick and mortar elysium... they established the rule, that all poor people should have the alternative (for they would compel nobody, not they) of being starved by a gradual process in the (work)house, or by a quick one out of it... They made a great many other wise and humane regulations..." (*Oliver Twist,* Penguin Classics edition, p. 55)

In the last stage of management of the British poor, the factory system of White slavery was instituted, the horrors of which were defended with the argument that its alternative was either the workhouse or enslavement overseas.

Inside the factory, death was by no means certain, and "self-respect" (conferred by the captains of industry), wages and sustenance could be obtained. Therefore, the factory system of White slavery was yet another "mercy," in the long history of "mercifully" substituting one form of enslavement of the British yeomanry for another and calling the process "progress" and "the advancement of civilization."

The advocates of all four of these systems of human organization have seldom argued their "merits" in comparison with the way of life offered the people by a traditional culture of craft-making and farming the land. To do so would be to compare the traditional rural existence of the White farmer and cottage handcraft-worker with the modern organization of the White working class. In such an analogy the evils of the latter would be overwhelmingly obvious.

Once land, the source of the independence of the British yeoman, had been removed, the resulting dependency attached to the White poor the station of servility, a process whose groundwork had been laid with the juridical defeat of ancestral peasant land claims as a result of the establishment of the concept of villein tenure in the 12th century; the consequences of which— evictions and enclosure— were not experienced on a mass scale until the Stuart era.

The attitude of the propertied classes toward the class of penurious Whites created by the avarice of the aristocracy, was expressed candidly by Joseph Townsend in his *A Dissertation on the Poor Laws* and by the Scottish magistrate Lord Braxfield in the 1793 trial of Thomas Muir.

Muir had been arrested for the "crime" of advocating the right to vote for White working men. At his trial, Braxfield ruled that, "Mr. Muir might have known that no attention could be paid (by parliament) to such a rabble (the White workers who had petitioned for voting rights). What right have they to representation?... A government in every country should be just like a corporation; and in this country it is made up of the landed interest, which alone has the right to be represented." (John F. Mackeson, *Bristol Transported,* p. 13).

Joseph Townsend argued both for the necessity of cheap White labor in boom economic times to relieve "delicate," rich people from the need to perform "drudgery," as well as for the elimination of the White "surplus poor" through starvation, during times of economic depression.

In good economic times, Townsend claimed that it was only natural that there should be destitute White people, "so that there may always be some to fulfill the most servile, the most sordid, and the most ignoble offices in the community... the stock of human happiness is thereby much increased, while the more delicate are... relieved from drudgery..." During economic downturns: "Some check, some balance, is therefore absolutely needful, and hunger is the proper balance."

This plutocratic ideology, systematized in the late 18th century, was not a new or minority view. It had been expressed before, but with more wit and cant. Now, what had previously been discussed only in councils of state and the drawing rooms of the aristocracy was printed in the open, for public circulation and approbation from the "high born."

The ideas of modernity and progress, with their Benthamite view of tradition as a toxic encumbrance, eclipsed the customary restraints of mercantilism with every glimmer of the coming of the machine age.

The doctrine of the inferiority of the White yeomanry and their expendability in the name of the cause of "advancing civilization," was formulated to a greater degree with the publication in 1798 of the Rev. Thomas R. Malthus' *An Essay of the Principle of Population* (greatly expanded and revised into two volumes in 1803). Malthus argued, "...it was pointless to provide relief for the poor, because this was a futile exercise, calculated simply to perpetuate their misery. He went further, denying that the (White) poor had any *right* to relief." (Inglis, p. 69).

Malthus reasoned that as long as hungry Whites received food from charity they would continue having more children. Malthus demanded "moral restraint" (celibacy) from impoverished married White couples who, because they were poor, had no right to have children, in his view. Their only "moral" course was self-extinction and with their eventual demise as a class, so too would poverty be extinguished, according to Maithus.

"Moral restraint, he argued, could operate among the poor only with very inconsiderable force, because the poor law removed the need for it, by offering allowances for children. Abolish the allowances, and the poor who exercised moral restraint would then be rewarded if they had no more children than they could afford—or better, no children at all." (Inglis, pp. 70-71).

Malthus provided the perfect solution to a problem which had long-haunted the British ruling class, the "surplus" White population who always presented the potential for revolutionary overthrow of the system of privilege. Their devaluation over the centuries, from villein to slave to pauper to felon had now reached its nadir. Those not gainfully employed would be starved to death, all for the "maximum good of society."

The political economist David Ricardo also advocated the starvation of unemployed Whites: "By engaging to feed all who may require food you in some measure create an unlimited demand for human beings... the population and the rates (taxes) would go on increasing in a regular progression until the rich were reduced to poverty..." (Inglis, pp. 149-150).

Here was the *raison d'etre* of the machine age. The factoryowners announced that they would take the White "refuse" doomed to otherwise starve and actually pay them. Thus was paved the way for the acceptance of factory slavery, celebrated as a mercy and the salvation of an otherwise bestial and valueless creature, the penurious White adult and child.

If this assessment appears to place too great an emphasis on what in retrospect, was merely a fleeting and aberrant 1790s dogma of an Industrial revolution which quickly disabused itself of such extreme plutocratic thinking, one may cite a book written in 1990 by Clemson University economist Clark Nardinelli, which attempts to make the case that the worst crime of the Industrial Revolution, the enslavement, maiming and death of five, six and seven year-old White children in factories, was, "given the circumstances" a "benefit" and an "opportunity..."

Nardinelli's book has been hailed as a major achievement and the definitive history of the period of the Industrial Revolution. This recent work takes the same attitude toward White child slaves as their 18th century factory overseers. The views of the robber barons are being celebrated in the 1990s as the historically correct response toward poor Whites.

In defending the enslavement of White children in factories, the professor writes, "An idyllic childhood devoted to education and play was simply not possible for most (White) children." (*Child Labor and the Industrial Revolution,* p. 156).[2]

One wonders what sort of reception Nardinelli and his university publisher would have received had he justified the enslavement of negro children in the antebellum South on the basis that an "idyllic childhood devoted to education and play was simply not possible for most Black children."

As we shall see, Nardinelli's *apologia* is part of a long line of both capitalist and supposedly "humanitarian" socialist thinkers for whom two different standards of morality have obtained: what qualified as oppression of negro slaves and what qualified as

---

[2] On p. 171 Nardinelli claims that Charles Dickens, "though a severe critic of child labor... did not write about child labor in any of his novels... with the exception of a brief... passage in *David Copperfield*..." Nardinelli is ignorant of the scene in *Oliver Twist,* wherein Oliver is slated to be apprenticed to a master of chimney-sweeps named Gamfield, whose countenance, Dickens informs us, "was a regular stamped receipt for cruelty." Oliver was initially sold to Gamfield for slightly more than £3, despite the fact that the master of sweeps "did happen to labor under the slight imputation of having bruised three or four boys to death already." A fortuitous turn of events caused the magistrate to void Oliver's chimney-sweep indentures at the last moment. "Few workhouse orphans were as fortunate as Oliver Twist to escape from the clutches of chimney-sweepers of Mr. Gamfield's ilk." (George L. Phillips, *England's Climbing Boys,* p. 4).

oppression for White ones—beginning with the fact that it has been ruled "improper" to even refer to White slaves as such, and concluding with economic arguments in favor of White enslavement which, were they to be advanced in precisely the same terms toward any other race of people, would be denounced as an egregious denial of fundamental human rights.

That such a denial of the rights of the White laborer and the violence done to those rights is still current and influential two hundred years after Bentham, Malthus, Ricardo and Townsend, illustrates the low status of White working and poor people even in our own time.

One may here argue that child labor in factories while repellent, was not slavery. Such an argument can only be based on a 20th century conception of a factory as a place merely of regimentation. The factories of the late 18th and early 19th centuries were very different establishments.

The Factory System

In 1830, the Rev. Richard Oastler, a Methodist minister in York, protested the conditions in the Bradford woolen mills where young children labored and were beaten if they fell asleep. Oastler attacked the hypocrisy of Yorkshire clergymen and politicians who condemned with great fervor the enslavement of Blacks in the West Indies while in England, "thousands of our fellow creatures... are this very moment... in a state of slavery more horrid than are the victims of that hellish system 'colonial slavery'... the very streets which receive the droppings of an 'Anti-Slavery Society' are every morning wet by the tears of innocent victims at the accursed shrine of avarice, who are compelled, not by the cartwhip of the negro slave-driver, but by the dread of the equally appalling thong, or strap, of the overlooker, to hasten, halfdressed, but not *half-fed,* to those magazines of British infantile slavery—the worsted mills in the town of Bradford!"

Oastler was publicly thanked by a delegation of English laborers at a meeting in York "...for his manly letters to expose the conduct of those pretended philanthropists and canting hypocrites who travel to the West Indies in search of slavery, forgetting there is a more abominable and degrading system of slavery at home." (Cecil Driver, *Tory Radical: The Life of Richard Oastler,* pp. 36-55; Inglis, p. 260).

White Slaves

The Industrial Revolution's factory labor force consisted primarily of White children from the workhouses who were seized and placed in the factories under a spurious indentured apprentice system:

"Here then was a ready source of labor—and a very welcome one. The children, provided with employment, would be rescued from pauperism; and the ratepayers (taxpayers) would be relieved of their part of the burden. So mill-owners began to appear in London, visiting parish officers, and making the necessary arrangements. The children were formally indentured as apprentices... What happened to them was nobody's concern. A parish in London, having got rid of a batch of unwanted pauper children, was unlikely to interest itself in their subsequent fate... The term 'apprenticeship' was in any case a misnomer..." (Inglis, pp. 75-76, 81).

"...many employers imported child apprentices, parish orphans from workhouses far and near. Clearly, overseers of the poor were only too keen to get rid of the orphans... children were brought (to the factories) like 'cartloads of live lumber' and abandoned to their fate... poor children, taken from workhouses or kidnapped in the streets of the metropolis, used to be brought down by... coach to Manchester and slid into a cellar in Mosley Street as if they had been stones or any other inanimate substance." (Marjorie Cruickshank, *Children and Industry*, pp. 13-14).

Being indentured as "pauper apprentices," children lost all ability to negotiate the terms of their bound labor. The term "apprentice" was a misnomer because they were not being taught a trade. Machine-tending was a custodial function, not a skill. A child labeled an indentured "apprentice" could be paid a pittance and forced to work the longest hours. For example, to induce free English adults to work a night shift at a factory would have cost the owners more in wages. These "disadvantageous terms" were avoided by compelling the enslaved children to work at night.

British children comprised a majority of the factory work force, "from two-thirds to three-quarters of the workers in the early factories... they were lucky if they earned a halfpenny an hour. For this they were made to work as children had never been made to work before" (Inglis, p. 104).

"...for the sake of a shilling a week ...at the age of five, children who had to be carried to work and who, once there, had to be terrorized to stay awake..." (Cruickshank, p. 20).

White Children worked up to sixteen hours a day and "During that period the doors were locked; children—and most of the mill workers were still children—were allowed out only 'to go to the necessary'... In some factories it was forbidden to open my of the windows; cotton fluff was everywhere, including on he children's food, but often, as they had to stand all day, they were too fatigued to have any appetite... The (child) apprentices who were on night shift might stay on it for as long as four or five years... although they were provided with dinner at midnight, the machinery did not stop (lnglis, pp. 80, 163, 164, 262).

This was labor without any breaks, "unceasing labor." When the children fell asleep at the machines, they were lashed into wakefulness with a whip alternately known as a thong or strap. If they arrived late to the factory, talked to another child or committed some other infraction they were beaten with an iron bar known as a billy-roller.

A contemporary witness described the factory children of Manchester, England as 'almost universally ill-looking, small, sickly, barefoot and ill-clad." (Edward Baines, *History of the Cotton Manufacture,* p. 462). Frances Trollope: "...in the room they entered, the dirty, ragged, miserable crew were all active in the performance of their various tasks; the overlookers, strap in hand, on the alert; the whirling spindles urging the little slaves who waited on them to movements as unceasing as their own." (*Michael Armstrong, Factory Boy*).

"...the essential feature of factory life, as it developed in England, was that the children were enslaved." (Inglis, p. 104).

Charles Shaw was a child laborer from the age of seven beginning in 1839. When an adult, he wrote a book about his experiences: "Fortunes were piled up on the pitiless toilings of little children, and thousands of them never saw manhood or womanhood. Their young life was used as tillage for the quick growth of wealth... I have seen sights of sickening brutality... these little White slaves were flogged at times as brutally, all things considered, as Legree flogged Uncle Tom. Nearly all England wept about thirteen years later for Uncle Tom, especially the 'classes,' but no fine lady or gentleman wept for the cruelly-used ...(English) children." (*When I Was a Child,* pp. 18, 22 and 65).

White children in the early factories were sometimes beaten to death, "killed by blows from overseers." (Cruickshank, p. 51).

Statement of Henry Dunn: "The overseer carries a strap... The boys are severely strapped... There was a tenter to every flat, and he was considered as a sort of whipper-in, to force the children to extra exertion... seen wounds inflicted upon children by tenters, by Alexander Drysdale, among others, with a belt or stick, or the first thing that came uppermost. Saw a kick given by the above-mentioned Alexander Drysdale, which broke two ribs of a little boy. Helped to carry the boy down to a surgeon. The boy had been guilty of some trifling offense, such as calling names to the next boy..."

Testimony of Ellen Ferrier, factory worker: "When Charles Kennedy was the overseer he licked us very bad, beat our heads... and kicked us very bad..."

Testimony of Mary Scott, factory worker: "Was here with Charles Kennedy... seen him strike Betty Sutherland; can't tell how often but it was terrible often..."

John Fortesque, an overseer at the Milne factory in Nottingham, England, gave the following statement: "There are some children so obstinate and bad they must be punished. A strap is used. Beating is necessary, on account of their being idle. We find it out this way: we give them the same number of bobbins each; when the number they ought to finish falls off, then they're corrected. They would try the patience of any man."

Statement from a Mr. Grant, a Manchester factory worker, April, 1833: "A child, not ten years of age, having been late at the factory one morning, had as a punishment, a rope put round its neck, to which a weight of twenty pounds was attached; and thus like a galley-slave it was compelled to labor..." (John C. Cobden, *The White Slaves of England,* pp. 121-122; 144-145).

Statement by Rev. Oastler, London, 1833: "In a mill at Wigan, the children, for any slight neglect, were loaded with weights of twenty pounds, passed over their shoulders and hanging behind their backs. Then there was a murderous instrument called a billy-roller, about eight feet long and one inch and a half in diameter, with which many children had been knocked down, and in some instances murdered by it." (*Times of London,* February 25, 1833).

An unknown writer expressed the bitter feelings of the early British factory workers:

"I'm up, but weary,
I scarce can reach the door,

And long the way and dreary—
Oh, carry me once more,
To help us we've no mother,
To live how hard we try—
They killed my little brother—
Like him I'll work and die!

The overlooker met her,
As to the frame she crept,
And with the thong he beat her,
And cursed her as she wept.
Alas, what hours of horror
Made up her latest day,
In toil and pain and sorrow,
They slowly passed away.

That night a chariot passed her,
While on the ground she lay;
The daughters of her master
An evening visit to pay,
Their tender hearts were sighing
As wrongs to negroes were told,
While the white slave was dying
Who gained their father's gold."
—*Birmingham Journal,* April 14, 1833.

"In *Bleak House* Dickens was to satirize evangelical 'telescopic philanthropy' in the person of Mrs. Jellyby, a do-gooder so absorbed in the welfare of the African natives of Borrioboola-Gha that she fails to notice her own family sinking into ruin. This was precisely Carlyle's point: with Irish... dying in ditches... it was the worst sort of rose-pink sentimentalism to worry oneself about West Indian negroes..." (Eugene R. August, introduction to Thomas Carlyle's *The Nigger Question,* Crofts Classics edition, p. xvii).

In the late 1830s William Dodd began his exhaustive research into the condition of the English poor. He estimated that in the year 1846 alone, 10,000 English workers, many of them children, had been mangled and mutilated by machinery or otherwise disabled for life. They were abandoned and received no compensation of any kind. Many died of their injuries.

"Among factory children themselves many suffered from scrofula, incipient consumption visible by the enlarged neck glands and white swellings of the joints. At best children who survived into adolescence outgrew the disease, though the deformities themselves persisted; in some cases, however, limbs had to be amputated and at worst children worked until they died." (Cruickshank, p. 30).

"...young children are allowed to clean the machinery, actually while it is in motion; and consequently the fingers, hands and arms are frequently destroyed in a moment. I have seen the whole of the arm, from the tip of the fingers to above the elbow, chopped into mince-meat, the cog-wheels cutting through the skin, muscles and in some places, through the bone... in one instance every limb but one was broken... (William Dodd, *The Factory System Illustrated,* pp. 21-22).

"Accidents were often due to... children being set to clean machinery while it was still in motion. The loss of two or three fingers was not exceptional. There were more serious accidents... such as that reported by a Stockport doctor in 1840 of a girl caught by the hair and scalped from the nose to the back of the head. The manufacturer gave her five shillings. She died in the workhouse." (Cruickshank, p. 51).

19th century factory worker William Dodd stated, "Petition after petition has been sent to the two houses of Parliament, to the prime minister, and to the Queen, concerning this unfortunate class of British subjects, but without effect. Had they only been black instead of white, their case would have been taken into consideration long ago."

The Rev. Charles Edwards Lester, the great-grandson of the Puritan theologian Jonathan Edwards, and later the American Consul in Italy, stated that if he had a choice between having his children born negro slaves in the South or poor people in England, he would choose the former: "I would sooner see the children of my love born to the heritage of Southern slavery than to see them subjected to the blighting bondage of the poor English operative's life." (Lester, *The Glory and the Shame of England,* vol. 1, p. viii).

"John Randolph of Roanoke, traveling in England and Ireland with his black manservant Johnny, wrote to a friend back home: 'Much as I was prepared to see misery in the south of Ireland, I was utterly shocked at the condition of the poor peasantry between Limmerick and Dublin. Why sir, John never felt so proud of being a Virginia slave. He looked with horror upon the mud hovels and miserable food of the white slaves, and I had no fear of his running away." (Cunliffe, p. 6).

Lest Americans imagine that such practices never darkened *our* shores, readers are referred to the documentary literature on White child labor in American factories, especially Markham, Lindsey and Creel's *Children in Bondage;* Ruth Holland's *Mill Child* and Lewis Hine's, *Photographs of Child Labor.*

By 1801, Samuel Slater's factory, one of the first built in America, employed over a hundred children. The oldest was ten, the youngest was four.

Theophilus Fisk, a Connecticut publisher and Jackson Democrat is ranked as one of the major leaders of the early U.S. labor movement. Fisk denounced wealthy White campaigners for negro rights and in 1836 gave what has been described as a "fierce anti-abolitionist speech" in South Carolina. Fisk's anger derived from his observation that *White* slavery had been ignored. Fisk "found that America's slaves had 'pale faces' and as abolitionism grew in Boston, called for an end to indulging sympathies for Blacks in the South and for 'immediate emancipation of the White (factory) slaves of the North." (Roediger, p. 75).

Charles Douglass, president of the New England Association of Farmers, Mechanics and Other Working Men, described the four thousand White children and women at work in the factories of Lowell, Massachusetts in the 1860s as "dragging out a life of slavery and wretchedness... These establishments (New England's factories) are the present abode of wretchedness, disease and misery..."

Ruth Holland, commenting on the participation of New England factory owners in the cause of abolitionism and rights for negroes in the south, observed, "It's a little difficult to believe that northern mill owners, who were mercilessly abusing (White) children for profit, felt such pure moral indignation at (negro) slavery." (*Mill Child,* p. 28).

Human Brooms

Thousands of White children in Great Britain were forced to work as human brooms inside chimney flues and led miserable lives and died horrid deaths. The condition of these chimneysweepers reveals perhaps more than other form of White slavery, the attitude of the ruling class toward the most defenseless and oppressed segment of the "surplus" White poor.

Chimney-sweeping had been practiced as a trade as far back as the Tudor era, but "the custom of forcing young boys to sweep flues with brushes and scrapers probably did not become general until the 18th century." British cities in the Georgian era were festooned with forests of rooftop brick and mortar. Several flues were usually installed in each of the chimneys of a Georgian mansion to satisfy the 18th century demand for more comfortable indoor heating— a fireplace in nearly every room being the new yardstick of comfort.

As the number of flues increased, their size decreased, the average being approximately ten by fourteen inches. Children were essential for their maintenance. The very architecture of Georgian England now reflected the throwaway status of the White pauper child. Like the White children enslaved in the factories, they had been recruited from the workhouses as "pauper apprentices":

"Parish officials... tried to get rid of pauper children as soon as they were old enough by apprenticing them to any master who would take them." These included the masters of chimneysweeps for whom thin, malnourished boys as young as four were considered ideal for their facility for entering narrow smoke channels.

An 18th century eyewitness to the system of child chimneysweeps, Jonas Hanway, stated that it was "equal to any of the miseries which human nature seems capable of supporting... and if the evil is suffered to reign any longer, it must level us with nations whom we call barbarians, if it does not ultimately draw down on us the vengeance of heaven." (*Improving the Lot of the Chimney Sweeps,* p. xxx).

Chimney sweeping "was often little more than thinly-disguised slavery." (Inglis, p. 30).

It was not uncommon to send the children up the chimneys while they were still on fire, or to place flaming straw in the grate, beneath a child who had entered the chimney but refused to go all the way up. Skeletal deformities and crippling were common, as were fatal accidents. An eyewitness accoun tells of a boy called to a job that needed to be done in haste. The child entered the flue but quickly came out again, saying it was too hot:

"The master told him to make as much haste as he could. He was a long time going up... heard him cry out he was hung to a nail; heard him crying and sobbing, very much; very near nine o'clock, having been up about twenty minutes; never heard anymore... Upon asking the boy's master... (he) sent another boy up after him; he went as far as he could reach his toes; the child said he could not pull him down, 'He won't come down, master,' who said, 'Damn him...

"The builder who extricated the boy said it was very difficult, as he was so wedged in, and the flue was so exceedingly hot. The flue was fourteen inches by twelve... That and the soot, and the heat, the builder testified, must have caused the boy's death by suffocation." (Inglis, pp. 136-137).

Those boys who escaped death often contracted cancer: "...in 1775... Percival Pott observed an overwhelming number of young chimney sweeps suffering from scrotal cancer. He believed that the horrendous disease in these malnourished boys, kept thin by their employers to fit down the chimneys, was caused by their constant exposure to soot... but the English government took more than fifty years to pass laws to protect them." (Marc Lappe, *Chemical Deception,* quoted in *E Magazine,* Sept.-Oct., 1991, p. 55).

In handbills and advertisements the masters of chimneysweeps would boast that they were in possession of "small boys" for the best work inside flues. "Little boys for small flues" was a popular advertising slogan.

An early 19th century investigation revealed that no child could be found who voluntarily entered the ranks of a sweep. They were all either orphans and indigents sold by the parish workhouses into servitude or they had been kidnapped, or sold by famished parents to a master of sweeps. The boys often had to be forced up the flues with slaps, kicks, beatings and sometimes, fire.

On Jan. 17, 1831, John Pasey, ten years of age, was sent up a flue at the Omnibus coffee-house. "It appears that the brick-work was decayed, and that when the boy had reached the top, the whole chimney gave way." The child was found with his skull crushed.

March, 1832: An eleven year old boy was ordered by his master, D. Casey, to ascend a smoke-filled chimney. The boy was afraid to enter it. "Casey, regardless of his natural apprehensions, beat him until he mounted." The lad suffocated to death.

Sept. 1, 1832: Michael Brien, apprentice chimney-sweep to Philip Corbett, "was engaged to sweep some chimneys in the house of George Barron, Esq. He arrived at Mr. Barron's about seven o'clock, and the kitchen fire having been lighted before that hour, Corbett said it would not be necessary to put out the fire for the purpose of sweeping the chimney, as he would cover it with slack... Having covered the fire with slack, he desired the boy to ascend the chimney and commence operations; the boy immediately obeyed, but before he proceeded many yards, cried out that the chimney was too hot to advance further.

"The master desired him to 'rattle away,' as the chimney was cool enough; the child continued to ascend with the greatest pain and difficulty... a tremendous blaze rushed up the chimney... the little sufferer succeeded in reaching the top of the chimney, and thence the roof of the house. A ladder was immediately procured, and the boy was brought down by Mr. Barron's servants. The appearance of the boy's body was truly distressing, having been dreadfully scorched and burned." He died about twelve hours later.

Oct. 10, 1832. A chimney-sweeper, "named William Cakebread, between six and seven years of age, was employed in sweeping an out-built flue at the back of the premises, No. 36, Oxford-street; when, from the rottenness of the brickwork, the whole fell with a tremendous crash into the backyard, just as he had reached the top, and buried him underneath masses of the brickwork and rubbish... on being taken to the Middlesex hospital, he survived only a few hours, when he expired in great agony."

Jan. 15, 1834. A small boy was inside a chimney when it burst into flames. "He was speedily conveyed to the hospital where he remained some time in a state of excruciating agony and died."

In May, 1839, a boy, William Wilson, was ordered to clean a flue that was still hot from a fire that had recently been extinguished. "He was grievously burned" and hospitalized "for weeks" during which he was described by a care-giver as a "meek, gentle, little creature... the tears started in his eyes when he was spoken kindly to." (Society for Superseding the Necessity of Climbing Boys, *The Trade of Chimney Sweeping*, pp. 2-20).

There are many such cases on record, commensurate with the investigations arising from the founding of reform societies in the early 19th century: "...newspaper accounts, reports of humane societies, and Parliamentary records contain hundreds of instances of climbing boys injured and killed, beaten and burned, deformed and diseased." (George L. Phillips, England's Climbing Boys, p. 4).

Since conditions were even worse before the trade came under scrutiny, it is fair to surmise that hundreds of equally fatal or harrowing cases dating from the 18th century went unreported.

It is no doubt difficult today to understand the rationale behind anyone sending a young child up a chimney while the fire was still lit in the grate. To grasp the mentality of the "higher orders" of the society of the time, it is necessary to appreciate the utter expendability of the lives of pauper White children as compared with the "necessity" of maintaining every luxury for the "high born."

One observer, writing in the *Edinburgh Review* in 1819 stated, "We come now to burning little chimney sweepers. A large party is invited to dinner— a great display is to be made; and about an hour before dinner, there is an alarm that the kitchen chimney is on fire! It is impossible to put off the distinguished personages who are expected. It gets very late for the soup and fish— the cook is frantic— all eyes are turned upon the sable consolation of the chimney sweep— and up into the midst of the burning chimney is sent one of the miserable infants of the brush."

Bills proposed in parliament requiring the abolition of the use of "climbing boys" under the age of ten, were defeated in the House of Lords in 1804, 1818 and twice in 1819. The Earl of Lauderdale argued against any restraint of the practices of the masters of the chimney-sweeps, on the basis that "children should be considered free agents for wage bargaining purposes."

Lord Milton declared the idea of outlawing the use of young children in the chimneys overly hasty since only very small children could possibly fit into the narrow flues. It would have required only a small expenditure by a homeowner to have the chimneys altered and widened to permit their cleaning by adults or machines, however.

Lord Sydney Smith sneered at the humanitarian appeals for saving the lives of White children impressed into chimney-sweeping. "Humanity," observed Smith "is a modern invention."

Lord Smith further stated that "such a measure (for the reform of the chimney-sweep trade), we are convinced from the evidence, could not be carried into execution without great injury to property." (*The Works of Sidney Smith,* vol. 2, p. 95).

In the English Parliament property rights were ruled paramount when legislation was proposed for preserving the lives and health of poor White children. Property rights were ruled to be of secondary consideration however, when the cause of emancipating negroes came to the fore. During this time, the atrocities visited upon the White children who climbed inside the chimneys of the wealthy was of little consequence compared with the massive attention given to the condition of the negroes of America.

"When Parliament abolished negro slavery in 1808, the flues of its august chambers were being climbed by boys four, five and six years of age, sold... to chimney sweepers for prices ranging from a few shillings to two guineas— the smaller the child, the better the price..." (George L. Phillips, p. 3).

David Ricardo, commenting upon the attempt to protect child laborers, wrote that "the legislature must not be allowed to infringe on the rights of the owners of property." (Inglis, p. 166). Unless, of course, that "property" was a Black slave, rather than a White one.

Where the enslaved White children who served as human brooms came to the attention of the public at all, it was usually in terms of drollery and the picaresque. The English essayist Charles Lamb painted a rosy picture of their sufferings, celebrating them as a kind of charming, aesthetic prop, a delightful spectacle of "almost clergy imps," decorating the roofs of London "from their little pulpits" (the tops of chimneys):

"In 1822 Charles Lamb's often quoted 'Praise for Chimney-Sweepers' appeared in the *London Magazine* to bring a smile to the reader's face as he noted the author's 'kindly yearning toward these dim specks— poor blots'... He could enjoy the whimsical scene of the shivering black-hued boy drinking his morning dish of saloop tea; to be amused by the little fellow, his 'poor red eyes, red from many a previous weeping, and soot inflamed'...

"Lamb, although successful in provoking a chuckle, did not attempt to bring a tear to the reader's eye. He might refer to the 'kibed heels,' the early-dawn working hours, the ragged and filthy clothes, the red-rimmed eyes; yet with the magic of romanticism he wove the facts of hardship and sorrow so deftly into the fanciful imagery, that the misery of the boys is softened and lost sight of, as if chimneysweepers and climbing boys had been translated to the world of Restoration comedies." (George L. Phillips, p. 31, Inglis, p. 167).

The most striking illustration of this upper-class attitude of depraved indifference to the agony of poor White children can be seen in the case of Mrs. Elizabeth Montagu, a very rich lady who took Lamb's "whimsy" to greater heights and, regarding herself as a "patroness" of London's penurious children, actually had extra chimneys constructed on her Sandleford Priory, "so that climbing-boys might have the pleasure of sweeping them" and she the pleasure of observing the children's "sport" (George L. Phillips, p. 31).

The lives of poor White children continued to be sacrificed even when machine-cleaning became feasible without alterations of any kind being made to flues. In 1828 Joseph Glass improved the design of a chimney-cleaning machine invented earlier by George Smart. The new modifications rendered the cleaning of every flue by means of the contrivance an inexpensive and efficient means of foregoing child labor for the purpose. The device was mostly ignored by the masters of sweeps and homeowners alike because English boys cost even less than the affordable cleaning-machine:

"...the cost of Glass' machine with a ball and brush amounted to £4; yet sweeps preferred boys whom they could easily obtain in almshouses or on the streets; they made the boys beg their food, so the upkeep was almost nothing. Whereas the machine was liable to wear and tear, the child was forced to work, often when he was ill; moreover the machine required the combined efforts of a master and journeyman; the child swept the chimney unaided." (George L. Phillips, p. 34).

"Is it possible," asked the reformer J.C. Hudson, "that women, whose love of infants is said to be so strong, can persist in employing little children for this purpose?" The answer was yes.

Samuel Roberts, in an 1834 essay on the boys used as chimney-sweeps, addressed his indignation toward the upper-class British females who met in their sumptuously-appointed parlors to weep with tender-hearted solicitude over the latest accounts from America of oppression to negroes, while in the next room, scarred and burned five year-old English boys enslaved as human brooms, were being forced up the lady's chimney without a thought for their welfare:

"There is a race of human beings in this country, the Chimney Sweepers' Climbing Boys... which... is more oppressed than the negroes in either the West Indian Islands, or in North America... These objects are *all* young and helpless. Their employment is tenfold more horrible than that of any attaching to the (negro) slaves... A far greater number of them are crippled, and rendered deformed for life. A far greater proportion of them die in consequence of hard usage, while the horrible deaths from suffocation, burning, and other accidents, are in this case, beyond measure more numerous. And all this at home, within our knowledge, before our eyes... in our very houses... How many of these poor infants... arrive at years of maturity?... of those who die young, who knows (or cares?) anything about them? The death of any of your favorite dogs would be more lamented..." (*An Address to British Females,* pp. 11-17).

Breaking the Chains of Illusion

Historian Oscar Handlin writes that in colonial America, White "servants could be bartered for a profit, sold to the highest bidder for the unpaid debts of their masters, and otherwise transferred like movable goods or chattels... In every civic, social and legal attribute, these victims of the turbulent displacements of the 16th and 17th centuries were set apart. Despised by every other order, without apparent means of rising to a more favored place, these men and their children, and their children's children seemed mired in a hard, degraded life... The condition of the first Negroes in the continental English colonies must be viewed within the perspective of these conceptions and realities of (White) servitude... ("Origins of the Southern Labor System," *William and Mary Quarterly,* April, 1950, p. 202).

The history of enslavement in America as portrayed in the tunnel vision of the corporate media has focused exclusively on the enslavement of negroes. The impression is given that only Whites bear responsibility for enslaving negroes and only negroes were slaves. In fact negroes in Africa as well as American Indian tribes such as the Cherokee engaged in extensive enslavement of negroes. The Cherokee Indians owned large plantations on which they worked their negro slaves in gangs (R. Halliburton, Jr., *Red over Black: Black Slavery among the Cherokee Indians,* p. 20).

White slaves were actually owned by negroes and Indians in the South to such an extent that the Virginia Assembly passed the following law in 1670: "It is enacted that noe negro or Indian though baptized and enjoyned their owne ffreedome shall be capable of any such purchase of christians..." (*Statutes of the Virginia Assembly,* Vol. 2, pp. 280-81).

Negroes also owned other negroes in America (Charleston County *Probate Court Records,* 1754-1758, p. 406).

While Whites languished in chains Blacks were free men in Virginia throughout the 17th century (*Willie Lee Rose, A Documentary History of Slavery in North America,* p. 15; John Henderson Russell, *Free Negro in Virginia, 1619-1865,* p.23; Bruce Levine, et al., *Who Built America?,* vol. I, p. 52).

In 1717, it was proposed that a qualification for election to the South Carolina Assembly was to be "the ownership of one white man." (*Journals of the Commons House of Assembly of the Province of South Carolina: 1692-1775,* volume 5, pp. 294-295).

Negroes voted in the Carolina counties of Berkeley and Craven in 1 706 "and their votes were taken." (Levine, p. 63).

Blacks were toting guns or other weapons and going about armed in the service of wealthy landowners at the same time that tens of thousands of enslaved White men were forbidden arms. In 1 678 one thousand negroes were armed by the planters and formed into a fighting militia for protection against the French (Carl and Roberta Bridenbaugh, *No Peace Beyond the Line: The English in the Caribbean, 1624-1690;* pp. 359-360).

In Carolina in 1704, 1707, 1712, 1738 and 1741 bills were passed authorizing armed negro militias in the service of the planters. In 1742 certificates were presented to the Black militiamen for services rendered. (Warren B. Smith, *White Servitude in Colonial South Carolina,* p. 98).

During the American Revolution, Lord Dunmore, the Royal Governor of Virginia appointed by the King, sought to win Virginia back for the British Crown with Black troops recruited in America, to be called the Ethiopian Regiment. Parties of Blacks in the South were armed by the British with guns, clubs and swords with the order to use them against rebellious American patriots. (Ronald Hoffman, "The Disaffected in the Revolutionary South," *The American Revolution: Explorations in the History of American Radicalism,* pp. 281-282).

"By the first of December (1775) nearly three hundred Blacks in uniform, with the words 'Liberty to Slaves' inscribed across their breasts, were members of Lord Dunmore's Ethiopian Regiment... On the ninth of December at the Battle of Great Bridge— the Lexington of the South—the British force of six hundred, nearly half Black, was thrown back by Woodford's (all-White, American) Second Virginia Regiment...

"In April, 1782, General Nathanael Greene informed Washington that the British had armed and put into uniform at least seven hundred Blacks. The Ethiopian Regiment was not the only Black unit. That same spring two members of a Black British cavalry troop, about a hundred strong, were killed in a skirmish (with patriots) at Dorchester, Virginia. Evacuating Boston, the royal army sailed to Halifax with a 'Company of Negroes.'... It is possible that tens of thousands of (Black) slaves in South Carolina and Georgia went over to the British... (Sidney Kaplan, *The Black Presence in the Era of the American Revolution, 1770-1800,* pp. 32, 61 and 67).

During the War of 1812, the British ranks included approximately three hundred armed American negroes, who were used in combat against American forces. Some of these negroes helped the British burn the White House in 1814 (Roediger, p. 44).³

No wonder that Frederic Douglass would declare to a White audience on Independence Day, nine years before the Civil War, "This Fourth of July is *yours,* not *mine.*"

The British aristocracy's penchant for arming negroes and Indians for combat against White Americans has largely been forgotten today, even though it was one of the factors which led the colonists to go to war against King George, and was cited as such in the Declaration of Independence. The patriots' outrage at Indian atrocities and anger at Dunmore's manumission of negroes, was summarized by Jefferson in one of the least quoted passages of the Declaration: "He (King George) has excited domestic insurrections amongst us (Dunmore's proclamation freeing Blacks in American jurisdiction), and has endeavored to bring on the inhabitants of our frontiers, the merciless Indian Savages, whose known rule of warfare, is an undistinguished destruction of all ages, sexes and conditions."

---

³ A few Blacks fought on the side of the Americans during the Revolution, including some Massachusetts negroes known as the "Bucks of America." The claim has long been made that the first victim of the British in the American Revolution was a Black, Crispus Attucks. In fact, Attucks was an Indian, a descendant of John Attucks, a Natick who had battled American pioneers in King Philip's War.

Poor Whites and the Southern Confederacy

Even if they attained their freedom, dirt-poor Whites were forced to compete against negro slave labor. Jobs were few and Southern planters sat idly as poor Whites died of malnutrition for want of food and medicine. Negro slaves were expensive. To protect their investments, White aristocrats usually treated their negro slaves well, providing for adequate food, clothing and medication even as poor Whites in the same town sickened and died from disease and malnutrition.

Try to envision the 19th century scene: yeoman southern Whites, sick and destitute, watching their children dying while enduring the spectacle of negroes from the jungles of Africa healthy and well-fed thanks to the ministrations of their fabulously wealthy White owners who cared little or nothing for the local "White trash."

In the course of an 1855 journey up the Alabama River on the steamboat Fashion, Frederic Law Olmsted, the landscape architect who designed New York's Central Park, observed bales of cotton being thrown from a considerable height into a cargo ship's hold. The men tossing the bales somewhat recklessly into the hold were negroes, the men in the hold were Irish. Olmsted inquired about this to a mate on the ship. 'Oh, said the mate, 'the niggers are worth too much to be risked here; if the Paddies are knocked overboard or get their backs broke, nobody loses anything." (Frederic Law Olmsted, *A Journey to the Seaboard Slave States,* pp. 100-101; G.E.M. de Ste. Croix, *Slavery and Other Forms of Unfree Labor,* p. 27).

In the antebellum South, "Gangs of Irish immigrants worked ditching and draining plantations, building levees and sometimes clearing land because of the danger to valuable (negro) slave property...George Templeton Strong, a Whig patrician diarist... considered Irish workmen at his home to have had 'prehensile paws' rather than hands. He denounced the 'Celtic beast'... Irish youths... were sometimes called 'Irish slaves' and more frequently 'bound boys'..." A common joke in the South in the pre-Civil War period was that when Blacks were ordered to work hard they complained that their masters were treating them 'like Irishmen.' (Roediger, pp. 133, 146,150).[4].

"When I was a boy,' recalled Waters Mcintosh, who had been a slave in Sumter, South Carolina, 'we used to sing, 'Rather be a nigger than a poor white man.' Even in slavery we used to sing that.'

---

[4] Strong's opinion was hardly unanimous. In the 1850s, Massachusetts legislator Caleb Cushing announced that he admitted "to an equality with me, sir, the White man— my blood and race—whether he be a Saxon of England or a Celt of Ireland... but I do not admit as my equals either the red man of America, or the yellow man of Asia, or the black of Africa"
Irish-Americans were among the foremost fighters for the rights of White workers and for separation of the races. The term *miscegenation* (from the Latin, *miscere,* to mix and *genus,* for race) was coined by two Irishmen, George Wakeman and D.G. Croly, in their anonymously written, 1863 anti-integration satire, *Miscegenation: The Theory of the Blending of the Races.* The Englishman James D. Burn observed that, "...it is in the Irish residents that they (American negroes) have, and will continue to have, their most formidable enemies..." (*Three Years Among the Working Classes in the U.S. During the [Civil] War,* p. xiv).

"Mr. McIntosh's remarks reveal... that the poor whites of the South ranked below blacks in social standing... slaves felt unbridled contempt for lower-class whites... Frederick Douglass opened his famous *Life and Times* with an account of Talbot County, Maryland, which he said housed a 'white population of the lowest order...

"Throughout the South the slaves of many of the larger planters lived in a society of blacks and wellto-do whites and were encouraged to view even respectable laboring Whites with disdain... Ella Kelly, who had been a slave in South Carolina:

"...You know, boss, dese days dere is three kind of people. Lowest down is a layer of white folks, then in de middle is a layer of colored folks, and on top is de cream, a layer of good white folks...

"The slaves noticed their masters sense of superiority toward marginal farmers as well as toward poor whites and, by associating themselves with 'de quality white folks,' strengthened their selfesteem...

"...a slave... expressed no surprise that his master, who was Big Buckra, never associated with white trash. And Rosa Starke, who had been owned by a big planter in South Carolina, reported that poor whites had to use the kitchen door when they went up to the Big House. Her mistress 'had a grand manner; no patience with poor white folks.'

"...The many (negro) ex-slaves who recalled the lot of the small farmers and poor whites as hard and even as bad as their own knew what they were talking about.

"...The slaves saw enough abject poverty, disease, and demoralization among the poor whites... to see their own condition under Ole Massa's protection as perhaps not the worst of evils." (Eugene D. Genovese, "Rather Be a Nigger Than a Poor White Man': Slave Perceptions of Southern Yeoman and Poor

Whites," in *Toward a New View of America,* pp. 79, 81-82, 84, 90-91).

This situation engendered a rage in the descendants and survivors of White slavery which has seldom been accounted for in the history of White working class support for the Northern abolitionist cause. We can gauge the attitude of yeoman Whites, especially in the border states like Kentucky and Tennessee, but throughout the U.S.A. as well, who were either neutral during the Confederacy's struggle or sided with Lincoln, from the statement of an Iowa Congressman who maintained that it was the planter aristocracy "which exalts and spreads Africans at the expense of the White race." (Emma Lou Thornbrough, "The Race Issue in Indiana Politics During the Civil War," *Indiana Magazine of History,* June, 1951).

Some of the leaders of the Free Soil Party and many of the Unionist soldiers who made up the ranks of Lincoln's armies in southern Ohio, western North Carolina, eastern Tennessee, southern Illinois, Kentucky and elsewhere were survivors of White slavery or descendants of White slaves. They did not view themselves as advocates of what was then referred to as racial "amalgamation." (2)

Historically they regarded themselves as separatists and viewed the Southern planter's desire to spread negroes into California, Oregon and other territories as a grave threat to free White labor and the Old Testament principle of racial separation (Nehemiah 13:23-27; Ezra 10:10-14; Hosea 5:7).

Congressman David Wilmot sponsored a law to ban Black slavery in the American West. He dubbed his proposed law, "the White Man's Proviso." He was bitterly opposed by the Southern elite. Wilmot told Congress that he intended to preserve

America's western frontier for "the sons of toil, my own race and color." (Charles B. Going, *David Wilmot: Free-Soiler,* p. 174).

During much of the Civil War the political and military leaders of the Confederacy could not travel in certain parts of the Deep South without armed escorts (Jeffrey Rogers Hummel, "The Civil War," *The United States at War Audio Classics Series,* Part Two), for fear of attack from "Upcountry" Southern Whites who hated the planter aristocracy and the war they saw as being for the sole benefit of the expansion of the planter's "infernal negroes." Upcountry Southern Whites consisted in large part of the survivors and the children of the survivors of White slavery who resided in the hills, mountains and Piedmont regions of the South under frontier conditions.

In the antebellum 19th century South, "A large number of white Southerners lived in the upcountry, an area of small farmers and herdsmen... engaged largely in mixed and subsistence agriculture... Little currency circulated, barter was common and upcountry families dressed in 'home-spun cloth, the product of the spinning wheel and the hand-loom.' This economic order gave rise to a distinctive subculture that celebrated mutuality, egalitarianism (for whites) and... independence.

"...mountain counties rejected secession from the outset. One citizen of Winston County in the northern Alabama hill country believed yeoman had no business fighting for a planter-dominated aristocracy: 'All tha want is to git you... to fight for their infernal negroes and after you do their fightin' you may kiss their hind parts for o tha care." (Eric Foner, *Reconstruction: America's Unfinished Revolution, 1863-1877,* pp. 11 and 13).

Poor Whites had to be drafted into the Confederate army. As in the North, where resistance to conscription was widespread, many Southern Whites saw the conflict as "a rich man's war and a poor man's fight." Indeed, any slaveholder owning 20 or more Black slaves was exempt from military combat.

From 1609 until the early 1800s, between one-half and two thirds of all the White colonists who came to the New World came as slaves. Of the passengers on the Mayflower, twelve were White slaves (John Van der Zee, *Bound Over,* p. 93). White slaves cleared the forests, drained the swamps, built the roads. They worked and died in greater numbers than anyone else.

Both psychologically and materially Whites in modern times are called upon to bear burdens of guilt and monetary reparation for negro slavery. This position is based entirely on enforced ignorance and the deliberate suppression of the record of White slavery in North America. Hundreds of thousands of Whites had been enslaved during the colonial era in America while millions of others were too poor to afford even a mule, much less a Black slave.

Slave reparations and guilty feelings are due— if one subscribes to such a thing as retroactive collective guilt— from the descendants of the minority of wealthy Whites who owned negro slaves and who, in the South at least, were themselves generally reduced to penury in the aftermath of the Civil War. Reparations would also have to be paid by the descendants of the Cherokee and other American Indian tribes who owned Black slaves and by the heirs of Black tribal leaders in Africa who sold them into slavery. (3)

Reparations must also be paid, if the logic of the situation is to be consistent, *to* the modern-day White descendants of the White slaves of early America.

The whole discussion of negro slavery, Southern racism and the Civil War as currently framed by the Establishment agenda, necessarily must exclude any examination of the fact of White slavery, especially in the 17th and 18th centuries, and the condition of free White poor in the 19th century forced to compete against negro slave labor in the South.

Whites Were the First Slaves in America

The enslavement of Whites extended throughout the American colonies and White slave labor was a crucial factor in the economic development of the colonies. Gradually it developed into a fixed system every bit as rigid and codified as negro slavery was to become. In fact, negro slavery was efficiently established in colonial America because Black slaves were governed, organized and controlled by the structures and organization that were first used to enslave and control Whites. Black slaves were "late corners fitted into a system already developed." (Ulrich B. Phillips, *Life and Labor in the Old South,* pp. 25-26).

White slavery was the historic base upon which negro slavery was constructed. "...the important structures, labor ideologies and social relations necessary for slavery already had been established within indentured servitude... white servitude... in many ways came remarkably close to the 'ideal type' of chattel slavery which later became associated with the African experience" (Hilary McD. Beckles, *White Servitude,* pp. 6-7 and 71). "The practice developed and tolerated in the kidnapping of Whites laid the foundation for the kidnapping of Negroes." (Eric Williams, *From Columbus to Castro,* p. 103).

The official papers of the White slave trade refer to adult White slaves as "freight" and White child slaves were termed "half-freight." Like any other commodity on the shipping inventories, White human beings were seen strictly in terms of market economics by merchants.

The American colonies prospered through the use of White slaves which Virginia planter John Pory delcared in 1619 were "our principall wealth."

"The white servant, a semi-slave, was more important in the 17th century than even the negro slave, in respect to both numbers and economic significance." (Marcus W. Jernegan, *Laboring and Dependent Classes in Colonial America,* p. 45).

Where mainstream history books or films touch on White slavery it is referred to with the deceptively mild-sounding title of "indentured servitude," the implication being that the enslavement of Whites was not as terrible or all-encompassing as negro "slavery" but constituted instead a more benign bondage, that of "servitude."

Yet the terms servant and slave were often used interchangeably to refer to people whose status was clearly that of permanent, lifetime enslavement. "An Account of the English Sugar Plantacons" (sic) in the British Museum (Stowe manuscript) written circa 1660-1685, refers to Black and White slaves as "servants": "...the Colonyes were plentifully supllied with Negro and Christian servants which are the nerves and sinews of a plantacon..." (Christian was a euphemism for White).

"In the North American colonies in the 17th and 18th centuries and subsequently in the United States, servant was the usual designation for a slave" (*Compact Edition of the Oxford English Dictionary,* p. 2,739).

The use of the word servant to describe a slave would have been very prevalent among a Bibleliterate people like colonial Americans. In all English translations of the Bible available at the time, from Wycliffe's to the 1 611 King James version, the word slave as it appeared in the original Biblical languages was translated as servant. For example, the King James Version of Genesis 9:25 is rendered: "Cursed be Canaan, a servant of servants shall he be." The intended meaning here is clearly that of slave and there is little doubt that in the mind of early Americans the word servant was synonymous with slave (cf. Genesis 9:25 in the New International Version Bible).

In original documents of the White merchants who transported negroes from Africa the Blacks were called servants: "...one notes that the Company of Royal Adventurers referred to their cargo as 'Negers,' 'Negro-Servants,' 'Servants... from Africa...' (Handlin, p. 205).

The documentary record debunks the propaganda that slavery was strictly a racist operation, part of a conspiracy of White supremacy, because: 1. Whites as well as Blacks were enslaved. 2. In the 17th century slaves of both races were called servants. 3. The colonial merchants of 17th century America had no qualms about enslaving their own White kindred. Oscar Handlin:

"Through the first three-quarters of the 17th century, the Negroes, even in the South, were not numerous... They came into a society in which a large part of the (White) population was to some degree unfree... The Negroes lack of freedom was not unusual. These (Black) newcomers, like so many others, were accepted, bought and held, as kinds of servants...

"It was in this sense that Negro servants were sometimes called slaves... For that matter, it also applied to white Englishmen... In New England and New York too there had early been an intense desire for cheap unfree hands, for 'bond slavery, villeinage or Captivity,' whether it be white, Negro or Indian..." (Handlin, pp. 202-203, 204, 218).

"The early laws against runaways, against drunkenness, against carrying arms or trading without permission had applied penalties as heavy as death to all servants, Negroes and Whites" (Handlin, p. 214).

A survey of the various ad hoc codes and regulations devised in the 17th century for the governing of those in bondage reveals no special category for Black slaves. (Hening, vol. 1, pp. 226, 258, 540).

"During Ligon's time in Barbados (1647-1650), white indentured female servants worked in the field gangs alongside the small but rapidly growing number of enslaved black women. In this formative stage of the Sugar Revolution, planters did not attempt to formulate a division of labor along racial lines. White indentured servants... were not perceived by their masters as worthy of special treatment in the labor regime." (Beckles, *Natural Rebels,* p. 29).

"...whiteness and independence were not firmly connected. Nor was Blackness yet fully linked with servitude." (Roediger, p. 27).

The contemporary academic consensus on slavery in America represents history by retroactive fiat, decreeing that conclusions about the entire epoch fit the characterizations of its final stage, the 19th century Southern plantation system. (4)

17th century colonial slavery and 19th century American slavery are not a seamless garment. Historians who pretend otherwise have to maintain several fallacies, the chief among these being the supposition that when White "servants" constituted the majority of servile laborers in the colonial period, they worked in privileged or even luxurious conditions which were forbidden to Blacks.

In truth, White slaves were often restricted to doing the dirty, backbreaking field work while Blacks and even Indians were taken into the plantation mansion houses to work as domestics:

"Contemporaries were aware that the popular stereotyping of (White) female indentured servants as whores, sluts and debauched wenches, discouraged their use in elite planter households. Many pioneer planters preferred to employ Amerindian women in their households... With the... establishment of an elitist social culture, there was a tendency to reject (White) indentured servants as domestics... Black women... represented a more attractive option and, as a result, were widely employed as domestics in the second half of the 17th century. In 1675 for example, John Blake, who had recently arrived on the island (of Barbados), informed his brother in Ireland that his white indentured servant was a 'slut' and he would like to be rid of her ...(in favor of a 'neger wench')." (Beckles, *Natural Rebels,* pp. 56-57).

In the 17th century White slaves were cheaper to acquire than Negroes and therefore were often mistreated to a greater extent.

Having paid a bigger price for the Negro, "the planters treated the black better than they did their 'Christian' white servant. Even the Negroes recognized this and did not hesitate to show their contempt for those white men who, they could see, were worse off than themselves..." (Bridenbaugh, p. 118).

It was White slaves who built America from its very beginnings and made up the overwhelming majority of stave-laborers in the colonies in the 17th century. Negro slaves seldom had to do the kind of virtually lethal work the White slaves of America did in the formative years of settlement. "The frontier demands for heavy manual labor, such as felling trees, soil clearance, and general infrastructural development, had been satisfied primarily by white indentured servants between 1627 and 1643." (Beckles, *Natural Rebels*, p. 8).

The merchant class of early America was an equal opportunity enslaver and viewed with enthusiasm the bondage of all poor people within their grasp, including their own White kinsmen. There was a precedent for this in the English legal concept of villeinage, a form of medieval White slavery in England.

"...as late as 1669 those who thought of large-scale agriculture assumed it would be manned not by Negroes but by servile Whites under a condition of villeinage. John Locke's constitutions for South Carolina envisaged an hereditary group of servile 'leetmmen'; and Lord Shaftsbury's signory on Locke Island in 1674 actually attempted to put the scheme into practice." (Handlin, p. 207).

The Random House Dictionary of the English Language defines servitude as "slavery or bondage of any kind." The dictionary defines "bondage" as "being bound by or subjected to external control." It defines "slavery" as "ownership of a person or persons by another or others."

Hundreds of thousands of Whites in colonial America were owned outright by their masters and died in slavery. They had no control over their own lives and were auctioned on the block and examined like livestock exactly like Black slaves, with the exception that these Whites were enslaved by their own race. White slaves "found themselves powerless as individuals, without honor or respect and driven into commodity production not by any inner sense of moral duty but by the outer stimulus of the whip." (Beckles, *White Servitude*, p. 5).

Upon arrival in America, White slaves were "put up for sale by the ship captains or merchants... Families were often separated under these circumstances when wives and offspring were auctioned off to the highest bidder." (Foster R. Dulles, *Labor in America: A History,* p. 7).

"Eleanor Bradbury, sold with her three sons to a Maryland owner, was separated from her husband, who was bought by a man in Pennsylvania." (Van der Zee, p. 165).

White people who were passed over for purchase at the point of entry were taken into the back country by "soul drivers" who herded them along "like cattle to a Smithfield market" and then put them up for auction at public fairs. "Prospective buyers felt their muscles, checked their teeth... like cattle..." (Sharon Salinger, *To Serve Well and Faithfully, Labor and Indentured Servants in Pennsylvania, 1682-1800,* p. 97). "...indentured servants were sold at auction, sometimes after being stripped naked." (Roediger, p. 30). "We were... exposed to sale in public fairs as so many brute beasts." (Ekirch, p. 129).

"Contemporary accounts likened them to livestock auctions. '(They) are brought in here,' a person noted, 'and sold in the same manner as horses or cows in our market or fair. (William) Green recalled:

'They search us there as the dealers in horses do those animals in this country, by looking at our teeth, viewing our limbs...'" (William Green, *Sufferings of William Green,* p. 6 and Ekirch, p. 123).

"They are frequently hurried in droves, under the custody of severe brutal drivers into the Back Country to be disposed of as servants." (Jernegan, p. 225).

Those Whites for whom no buyer could be found even after marketing them inland were returned to the slavetrader to be sold for a pittance. These Whites were officially referred to as "refuse" and "lumps": "Unloading large numbers wholesale, called 'lumping,' was generally a last resort that yielded smaller rewards."

White slaver James "Cheston wrote to his partners, 'The servants go off slower than I expected... I shall try them a few days longer in the retail way and then lump the remainder.

"Large-scale purchasers generally retailed servants farther inland.... 'They drive them through the country like a parcel of sheep until they can sell them to advantage," wrote White slave John Harrower.

The Virginia Company arranged with the City of London to have 100 poor White children "out of the swarms that swarme in the place" sent to Virginia in 1619 for sale to the wealthy planters of the colony to be used as slave labor. The Privy Council of London authorized the Virginia Company to "imprison, punish and dispose of any of those children upon any disorder by them committed, as cause shall require." (Emphasis supplied).

The trade in White slaves was a natural one for English merchants who imported sugar and tobacco from the colonies. Whites kidnapped in Britain could be exchanged directly for this produce. The trade in White slaves was basically a return haul operation.

The operations of Captain Henry Brayne were typical. In November of 1670, Capt. Brayne was ordered to sail from Carolina with a consignment of timber for sale in the West Indies. From there he was to set sail for London with a load of sugar purchased with the profits from the sale of the timber. In England he was to sell the sugar and fill his ship with from 200 to 300 White slaves to be sold in Carolina.

The notion of a "contract" and of the legal status of the White in "servitude" became a fiction as a result of the exigencies of the occasion. In 1623 George Sandys, the treasurer of Virginia, was forced to sell the only remaining eleven White slaves of his

Company for lack of provisions to support them. Seven of these White people were sold for 150 pounds of tobacco.

The slave-status of Whites held in colonial bondage can also be seen by studying the disposition of the estates of the wealthy Whites. Whites in bondage were rated as inventories and disposed of by will and by deed along with the rest of the property. They were bought, sold, bartered, gambled away, mortgaged, weighed on scales like farm animals and taxed as property.

Richard Ligon, a contemporary eyewitness to White slavery, in his 1657 *A True and Exact History* tells of a White slave, a woman, who was being traded by her master for a pig. Both the pig and the White woman were weighed on a scale. "The price was set for a groat a pound for the hog's flesh and six pence for the woman's flesh..." (p. 59).

In general, Whites were not treated with the relative dignity the term "indentured servants" connotes, but as degraded chattel—part of the personal estate of the master and on a par with his farm animals.

The term "indentured servitude" therefore is nothing more than a propagandistic softening of the historic experience of enslaved White people in order to make a false distinction between their sufferings and those of negro slaves.

This is not to deny the existence of a fortunate class of Whites who could in fact be called "indentured servants" according to the modern conception of the term, who worked under privileged conditions of limited bondage for a specific period of time, primarily as apprentices. These lucky few were given religious instruction and could sue in a court of law. They were employed in return for their transportation to America and room and board during their period of service.

But certain historians pretend that this apprentice system-the privileged form of bound labor—was representative of the entire experience of White bondage in America. In actuality, the indentured apprentice system represented the condition of only a tiny segment of the Whites in bondage in early America.

"Strictly speaking, the term indented servant should apply only to those persons who had bound themselves voluntarily to service but it is generally used for all classes of bond servants." (Oliver P. Chitwood, *A History of Colonial America,* p. 341).

Richard B. Morris in *Government and Labor in Early America* notes that, "In the colonies, however, apprenticeship was merely a highly specialized and favored form of bound labor. The more comprehensive colonial institution included all persons bound to labor for periods of years as determined either by agreement or by law, both minors and adults, and Indians and Negroes as well as whites" (p. 310).

In a reversal of our contemporary ideas about White "indenture" and Black "slavery," many Blacks in colonial America were often temporary bondsmen freed after a period of time. Peter Hancock arranged for a negro servant named Asha to serve for twelve months, thenceforth to be a free person. (Bridenbaugh, pp. 120-121). Black indentured servants in the 18th century even had an "education clause" in their contracts:

"...free negro boys bound out as apprentices were sometimes given the benefit of an educational clause in the indenture. Two such cases occur in the Princess Anne County Records; one in 1719, to learn the trade of tanner, the master to 'teach him to read,' and the other, in 1727, to learn the trade of gunsmith, the master to teach him 'to read the Bible distinctly." (Jernegan, p. 162).

Newspaper and court records in South Carolina cite "a free negro fellow named Johnny Holmes... lately an indented servant with Nicholas Trott..." and "a negro man commonly called Jack Cutler— he is a free negro having faithfully served out his time with me four years according to the contract agreed upon..." (Warren B. Smith, p. 106).

David W. Galenson is the author of an Orwellian suppression of the horrors and conditions of White slavery entitled *White Servitude in Colonial America.* He states concerning White slaves, "European men and women could exercise choice both in deciding whether to migrate to the colonies and in choosing possible destinations."

This is positively misleading. At the bare minimum, hundreds of thousands of White slaves were kidnapped off the streets and roads of Great Britain in the course of more than one hundred and fifty years and sold to captains of slaveships in London known as "White Guineamen."

Ten thousand Whites were kidnapped from England in the year 1670 alone (Edward Channing, *History of the United States,* vol. 2, p. 369). The very word "kidnapper" was first coined in Britain in the 1600s to describe those who captured and sold White children into slavery ("kid-nabbers").

Another whitewash is the heralded "classic work" on the subject, Abbot Emerson Smith's *Colonists in Bondage* which is one long coverup of the extent of the kidnapping, the denial of the existence of White slavery and numerous other apologies for the establishment including a coverup of the deportation and enslavement of the Irish people. But the record proves otherwise. (For more on Abbot Emerson Smith's errors cf. Warren B. Smith, *White Servitude in Colonial South Carolina,* p. ix).

Irish Slaves

"Cromwell's conquest of Ireland in the middle of the seventeenth century made slaves as well as subjects of the Irish people. Over a hundred thousand men, women and children were seized by the English troops and shipped to the West Indies, where they were sold into slavery..." (George Novack, "Slavery in Colonial America," *America's Revolutionary Heritage,* p. 142).

On Sept. 11, 1655 came the following decree from the Puritan Protectorate by Henry Cromwell in London:

"Concerning the younge (Irish) women, although we must use force in takinge them up, yet it beinge so much for their owne goode, and likely to be of soe great advantage to the publique, it is not in the least doubted, that you may have such number of them as you thinke fitt to make use uppon this account." The "account" was enslavement and transportation to the colonies.

A week later Henry Cromwell ordered that 1,500 Irish boys aged 12 to 14 also be shipped into slavery with the Irish girls in the steaming tropics of Jamaica and Barbados in circumstances which killed off White adult slaves by the thousands due to the rigors of field work in that climate and the savage brutality of their overseers. In October the Council of approved the plan.

Altogether more than one hundred thousand Irish were shipped to the West Indies where they died in slavery in horrible conditions. Children weren't the only victims. Even eighty year old

Irish women were deported to the West Indies and enslaved (D.M.R. Esson, *The Curse of Cromwell: A History of the Ironside Conquest of Ireland,* 1649-53, p. 176).

Irish religious leaders were herded into "internment camps throughout Ireland, and were then moved progressively to the ports for shipment overseas like cattle." (D.M.R. Esson, p. 159). By the time Cromwell's men had finished with the Irish people, only one-sixth of the Irish population remained on their lands. (Esson, p. 168).

Protestant Slaves

Cromwell did not only enslave Catholics. Poor White Protestants on the English mainland fared no better. In February, 1656 he ordered his soldiers to find 1,200 poor English women for enslavement and deportation to the colonies. In March he repeated the order but increased the quota to "2,000 young women of England." In the same year, Cromwell's Council of State ordered all the homeless poor of Scotland, male and female, transported to Jamaica for enslavement (Eric Williams, p. 101).

Of course, Cromwell and the Puritan ruling class were not the only ones involved in the enslavement of Whites. During the Restoration reign of King Charles II, the monarch with Catholic sympathizers who had been Cromwell's arch-enemy, the king enslaved large groups of poor Presbyterians and Scottish Covenanters and deported them to the plantations in turn.

Legislation sponsored by King Charles II in 1686, intended to ensure the enslavement of Protestant rebels in the Caribbean colonies, was so harsh that one observer noted, "The condition of these Rebels was by this Act made as bad, if not worse than the Negroes." (Richard Hall, *Acts Passed in the Island of Barbados,* p. 484).

"By far the largest number and certainly the most important group of white indentured servants were the poor Protestants from Europe." (Warren B. Smith, p. 44).

Legal Basis and Definitions

In the late 16th century the English parliament empowered magistrates to enslave the British poor, "beyond the seas." In 1615 James I gave similar authorization. The operation was formalized with the passage of the Transportation Act of 1718, the preamble of which declared "...that its purpose was both to deter criminals and to supply the colonies with labor. Since 'in many of His Majesty's colonies and plantations in America there is a great want of servants..." (A.G.L. Shaw, *Convicts and the Colonies,* p. 25).

One of the earliest advocates of the enslavement of indigent Whites for labor in *Nova Britannia* was the Elizabethan preacher and geographer Richard Hakluyt, who advised the Crown that poor Whites should be "condemned for certain years in the western parts" (of the New World) where they would "be raised again, and do their country good service' by performing such useful chores as felling timber, mining precious minerals and raising sugar cane." (Richard Hakluyt, *A Discourse Concerning Western Planting* [Deanne edition], p. 37; A. Roger Ekirch, Bound for America, p. 7).

Hakluyt was among the first to label the new British poor, "criminals" and to urge their utilization as slave laborers in America, a process which would later become known under the euphemism, "transportation." (A.L. Rowse, *The Elizabethans and America,* p. 46).

Confronted with the labor shortage typical in early America, the colony of New York petitioned for White slaves from England in 1693. The Quakers of Philadelphia also sought them. (Shaw, pp. 32-34).

There were four categories of status for White people in colonial America: White freemen, White freemen who owned property, White apprentices (also called "indentured servants," "redemptioners" and "free-willers") and White slaves.

The attempt by Abbot Emerson Smith, Galenson and many others to deny the existence and brutal treatment of White slaves by pretending they were mostly just "indentured servants" learning a trade, regulated according to venerable, medieval Guild traditions of apprenticeship, runs completely counter to the documentary record.

"…the planters did not conceive of their (White) servants socially and emotionally as integral parts of the family or household, but instead viewed them as an alien commodity… Having abandoned the moral responsibility aspect of pre-capitalist ideology, masters enforced an often violent social domination of (White) servants by the manipulation of oppressive legal codes… transform(ing)… indentured servitude, with its pre-industrial, moral, paternalistic superstructure, into a market system of brutal servitude… maintained by the systematic application of legally sanctioned force and violence." (Beckles, *White Servitude,* pp. xiv and 5).

Informal British and colonial custom validated the kidnapping of working-class British Whites and their enslavement in the colonies under such euphemisms as "Servitude according to the Custom," which upheld the force of "verbal contracts" which shipmasters and press-gangs claimed existed between them and the wretched Whites they kidnapped off the streets of England and sold into colonial slavery.

These justifications for White slavery arose in law determined by penal codes. In other words, White slavery was permitted and perpetuated on the claim that all who were thus enslaved were criminals. No proof for this claim was needed because the fact of one's enslavement "proved" the fact of one's "criminality." The history of White slavery in the New World can be found within the history of the enforcement of the penal codes in Britain and America.

The "convicts," once in America, "...encountered widespread exploitation. Tobacco planters... felt few qualms about putting freeborn Englishmen to hard labor or, if need be, shackling them in chains. Neither the status of convicts as servants nor their living conditions were altogether different from those of slaves, and opportunities for achieving a settled social life were arguably worse." (Ekirch, pp. 3-4).

"Punctilious' gentlemen 'disdain that Englishmen should be slaves on *English* land,' a correspondent in the *Gentleman's Magazine* pointed out, 'and rather choose America for the theatre of *our* shame." (Ekirch, p. 21).

The claim of the aristocracy that these "convicts" were mainly dangerous criminals and felons guilty of heinous crimes, was largely a function of the propaganda that attended the enterprise of White slavery in the early American era: "...the great bulk of offenses were committed, not by professional thieves, but by the needy poor..." due to what one witness, the clergyman Francis Hare, described as "the extreme misery and poverty great numbers are reduced to." (Ekirch, p. 13).

Slaves were made of poor White "criminals" who had poached a deer, stolen a loaf of bread or had been convicted of destroying shrubbery in an aristocrat's garden. In 1 655 four teenagers were whipped through the streets of Edinburgh, Scotland, burned behind the ears and "barbadosed" into slavery in the colonies for interrupting a minister, James Scott, while he was preaching in church. (*Calendar of State Papers, Colonial Series, America and West Indies,* volume 5).

Under British law in the 17th and 18th centuries, "felonies" punishable by death included stealing or vandalizing gates, fruits, canal-banks and hop-binds. Other capital crimes included breaking down the head of a fish-pond, 'whereby fish may be lost,' cutting down trees in an avenue or garden, sending threatening letters, selling cotton with forged stamps and committing "sacrilege." (Shaw, pp. 26-27). Crimes punishable by transportation into slave labor in America included: stealing ore from lead mines, fishing in enclosed ponds, bigamy, and solemnizing a marriage in secret (Shaw, p. 27)[5].

A "felon" was a pregnant, starving woman who stole a bowl of soup; a 12 year old boy who had picked someone's pocket, or a young father like Thomas Atwood with a wife, child and mother to support, sentenced to slavery in America because he had stolen a sheep to satisfy the "cries of his family for bread at a time when he had it not to give them" (Ekirch, pp. 27-28, 50, 67).

---

[5] Unfortunately there tended to be one law for the rich and another for the poor. Eldon's confession in the House of Lords in 1827 that as a boy he had been a 'great poacher' was greeted with laughter. Working class English children were transported into slavery for stealing apples from a tree, a "crime" which "was committed almost daily by most of the high-born youths of the country" without fear of punishment. (Shaw, p. 163).

They would be separated from their parents, children or spouse and "transported" to the colonies, often for life.

Catherine Davis, a pregnant seamstress, was convicted in a London court of stealing seven yards of lace. She was separated from her husband, sentenced to slavery and placed aboard the convict ship Forward. She gave birth on board. Her baby was dead within two weeks, its mother bound for Maryland. (Ekirch, p. 111).

Awaiting a slave ship in a Cambridge, England jail, the "convict" Mary Featherstone, charged with theft, gave birth to a baby boy. He was taken from her and she was transported to slavery in His Majesty's Plantations in America. (Ekirch, p. 8).

"Laboring men often suffered abusive treatment in the colonies, but transported felons made especially easy prey. Marked with the stamp of infamy... 'Worse than negroes,' in fact, was the verdict of a Jamaican governor... many convicts were already viewed in much the same way as slaves... convict servants... toiled under debased conditions not altogether different from black slavery... Some observers, in fact, held that convicts suffered harsher treatment... 'Like horses you must slave, and like galley-slaves will you be used" (Ekirch, pp. 140, 151, 156, 160).

The "convict" label was so ubiquitous that it prompted Samuel Johnson's remark on Americans: "Sir, they are a race of convicts, and ought to be content with anything we allow them short of hanging."

But even an exclusive focus on the indentured servant or "apprentice" class cannot conceal the fact of White slavery because very often the distinctions between the two blurred:

"Large companies did not deal solely in convicts. Some participated in the indentured servant trade, so that servants and convicts were at times transported on the same ships... Eddis claimed that planters 'too generally conceive an opinion that the difference is merely nominal between the indented servant and the convicted felon'... another believed that they (indentured servants) 'are obliged to serve like slaves or convicts, and are on the same footing'... such observations do afford tantalizing evidence that some (White) servants were gradually becoming associated, in the public mind, with convicts, and, further, that many convicts were already viewed in much the same way as slaves." (Ekirch, pp. 75 and 156).

Through a process of subterfuge and entrapment, White apprentices were regularly transformed into White slaves, as we shall see.

White slaves were owned not only by individual aristocrats and rich planters but by the colonial government itself or its governor. White slaves included not just paupers but such "wicked villaines" as "vagrants, beggars, disorderly and other dissolute persons" as well as White children from the counties and towns of Britain who were stolen from their parents though no Harriet Beecher Stowe rose to prominence in chronicling the anguish and hardship of these enslaved White children.

White Political Prisoners Sold into Slavery

A large number of the White slaves arriving in America described as "convicts" were actually political prisoners. Of the Scottish troops captured at the battle of Worcester more than 600 hundred were shipped to Virginia as slaves in 1651. The rebels of 1666 were sent as slaves to the colonies as were the Monmouth rebels of 1 685 and the Jacobites of the rising of 1715.

"It is now commonly accepted that the African slave trade could not have operated for over three centuries without the active participation of some African states and political leaders. The human merchandise was obtained largely as a result of political conflicts between neighboring states and tribes.

"Less well known are the ways in which... (White slave laborers were obtained)... from the British Isles for the West Indies plantations in the seventeenth century. The English state ruthlessly rounded up victims of political conflict and prisoners of war at places like Dunbar, Worcester, Salisbury and, during territorial expansionism, in Ireland, for sale to West Indian merchants. In this respect English governments and African political leaders were responding to the same market forces." (Beckles, *White Servitude,* p. 52).

The Crown put tens of thousands of political dissidents in slavery, some being shipped to New England while others were deported to the plantations of the West Indies and worked to death in the island's boiler houses, mills and sugar cane fields. Cromwell sold the White survivors of the massacre at Drogheda to slave-traders in the Barbados "and thereafter it became his fixed policy to 'barbadoes' his opponents" (Eric Williams, p. 101).

By 1655, half of the total White population of Barbados consisted of political prisoners sold into slavery (Jill Sheppard, *The 'Redlegs' of Barbados,* p.18).

Establishment historians claim that only Blacks were slaves because Whites were released after a term of seven or ten years of servitude. But the history of the enslavement of Britain's political prisoners disproves this notion. Plantation owners saw it as their profitable and patriotic duty to extend the servitude of the political prisoners on the plantations far beyond the supposed ten or twenty year limit.

British political prisoners were shipped into slavery in America for life, not seven or fourteen years: "...those who survived the voyage worked out their lives in bondage on the plantations of America." (John Prebble, *Glencoe,* p. 65).

"After the battle of Worcester in 1652 the first mention is made of Royalists having been brought out to Barbados and sold as slaves... they had been taken prisoner at Exeter and Ilchester... From there they were driven straight to Plymouth, put on a ship where they remained below deck, sleeping amongst the horses. On arrival in Barbados they were sold as chattel and employed in grinding the mills, attending to the furnaces and digging in the hot sun—whipped at the whipping post as rogues, and sleeping in sties worse than pigs." (Ronald Tree, *A History of Barbados,* p. 35).

This was no "temporary bondage." Of 1300 Cavaliers enslaved in 1652 in Barbados almost all of them *died* in slavery.

(Bridenbaugh, pp. 110-111; Heinrich von Uchteritz, *Kurze Reise,* pp. 3-10).

The enslavement of White political prisoners in the West Indies was debated in the English Parliament on March 25, 1 659. The practice was allowed to continue and was still in operation as late 1746 when Scottish Highland infantrymen and French and Irish regulars of the Jacobite army were transported into slavery in Barbados after the battle of Culloden. (Sheppard, p. 3).

Slave Hunting in Britain

Whites convicted of no crime whatever were made slaves by being captured by press-gangs in Britain and shipped into slavery in colonial America. These slave raids (also known as "spiriting"), began under the reign of King Charles I, continued during the Commonwealth period and throughout the reign of Charles II. It was an organized system of kidnapping English, Welsh and Scottish workers, young and old, and transporting them to the American colonies to be sold, with the profits split between the press-gangs and the shipmaster to whom the captured Whites were assigned in chains.

These slave hunting gangs were viewed with covert approval by the British aristocracy who feared the overpopulation of the White underclass. Confiscatory levels of taxation and the enclosure laws had driven British small farmers and village dwellers off the land and into the cities where they gathered and "loitered," a threat to the order and comfort of the propertied classes.

17th and 18th century economists advocated the enslavement of poor Whites because they saw them as the cheapest and most effective way to develop the colonies in the New World and expand the British empire. It was claimed that by making slave laborers out of poor Whites they were saved from being otherwise, "chargeable and unprofitable to the Realm."

As the plantation system expanded in the southern American colonies, planters demanded the legalization of the practice of kidnapping poor Whites. As it stood, laws were on the books forbidding kidnapping, but these were for show and were enforced with very infrequent, token arrests of "spirits." The planters' need for White slave labor expanded to such an extent that they tired of having to operate in a quasi-legal manner.

In response in February, 1652 it was enacted that:

...it may be lawful for... two or more justices of the peace within any county, citty or towne corporate belonging to this commonwealth to from tyme to tyme by warrant... cause to be apprehended, seized on and detained all and every person or persons that shall be found begging and vagrant... in any towne, parish or place to be conveyed into the port of London, or unto any other port... from where such person or persons may be shipped... into any forraign collonie or plantation..." (*Egerton manuscript,* British Museum).

Parliamentary legislation of 1664 allowed for the capture of White children who were rounded up and shipped out in chains. Judges received 50% of the profits from the sale of the White youths with another percentage going to the king.

With these laws, it was open season on the poor of Great Britain as well as anyone the rich despised. In 1 682 four White men from Devon, England were enslaved and transported to the colonies. The judges had indicted the four for "wandring." From 1 662 to 1665, the judges of Edinburgh, Scotland ordered the enslavement and shipment to the colonies of a large number of "rogues" and "others who made life unpleasant for the British upper classes" (*Register for the Privy Council of Scotland,* third series, vol. 1, p. 181; vol. 2, p. 101).

Scottish royalty had tenant farmers to whom they owed money, kidnapped and sold to slavers under the pretense that they had been ordered for transportation to the colonies as convict slave-laborers. 'It has been whispered, Edward Burt affirmed, "their crimes were only asking their dues..." (Edward Burt, *Letters from a Gentleman*, vol. I, pp. 54-55).

In 1739, "Under the orders of two lairds on the Isle of Skye, Sir Alexander MacDonald and Norman MacLeod, over 100 men, women and children were kidnapped one evening from their homes on Skye and several neighboring islands.

As one of the victims later recounted, they were 'all guarded and delivered... and a good deal of them were at the same time bound and tied.' The plan was to ship the prisoners to either New England or Pennsylvania, where they would be sold as servants, but when the vessel stopped to take on supplies at Donaghadie, in Northern Ireland, they escaped across the surrounding countryside... neither MacDonald or MacLeod was ever prosecuted." (Ekirch, p. 32).

In Charles County court in Maryland in 1690 it was agreed that the "indentures" under which seven White slaves were being held were "kidnapper's indentures" and therefore technically invalid. However, the court ruled that the White slaves should continue to be held in slavery to their various colonial masters based on the so-called "custom of the country."

The ladies of the royal court and the mayor of Bristol, England were not beneath profiting from the lucrative traffic in poor White people. Every pretense was used to decoy the victims aboard ships lying in the Thames. The kidnapping of poor Whites became a major industry in such English port cities as London, Plymouth, Southampton and Dover and in Scotland at Aberdeen where the kidnapping of White children and their sale into slavery "had become an industry."

White Children in Chains

The kidnapping of English children into slavery in America s actually legalized during the first quarter of the 17th century. In that period a large number of the children of poor parents, as well as orphan children, were targeted for the White slave trade. These poor White children were described as a "plague" and a "rowdy element."

Aristocrats who ran the Virginia Company such as Sir Thomas Smythe and Sir Edwin Sandys viewed the children as a convenient pool of slave laborers for the fields of the Virginia colony. In their petition to the Council of London in 1618 they complained of the great number of "vagrant" children in the streets and requested that they might be transported to Virginia to serve as laborers.

A bill was passed in September of 1 61 8 permitting the capture of children aged eight years old or older, girls as well as boys. The eight year old boys were to be enslaved for sixteen years and the eight year old girls for fourteen years, after which, it was said, they would be given land. (Robert C. Johnson, "The Transportation of Vagrant Children from London Virginia, 1618-1622," in *Early Stuart Studies,* p. 139).

A directive was issued for the capture of children in London, empowering city aldermen to direct their constables to seize children on the streets and commit them to the prison-hospital at

Bridewell, where they were to await shipment to America (Johnson, pp. 139-140). "...their only 'crime' was that they were poor and happened to be found loitering or sleeping in the streets when the constable passed by." (Johnson, p. 142).

The street was not the only place child slaves were to be procured however. The homes of indigent parents with large families were also on the agenda of the slave-traders. Poor English parents were given the "opportunity" to surrender one or more of their children to the slavers. If they refused they were to be starved into submission by being denied any further relief assistance from the local government:

"To carry out the provisions of the act the Lord Mayor (Sir William Cockayne)... directed the alderman ...to (make) inquiry of those parents 'overcharged and burdened with poor children' whether they wished to send any of them to Virginia... those who replied negatively were to be told they would not receive any further poor relief from the parish." (Johnson, p. 142).

The grieving parents were assured that the shipment of their children to Virginia would be beneficial to the children because it was a place where 'under severe masters they may be brought to goodness." (Johnson, p. 143).

In January of 1620 a group of desperate, terrified English children attempted to break out of Bridewell where they had been imprisoned while awaiting the slave-ships to America. They rose up and fought:

"...matters were further complicated by the refusal of some of the children to be transported. In late January a kind of 'revolt' occurred at Bridewell, with some of the 'ill-disposed' among the children declaring 'their unwillingness to go to Virginia...'" (Johnson, p.143).

"A hasty letter from (Sir Edwin) Sandys to the King's secretary (Sir Robert Naunton) quickly rectified the situation." On January 31 the Privy Council decreed that if any of the children continued in their "obstinance" they would be severely punished. It is possible that one of the children was actually executed as an example to the others. What is certain is that a month later the children, mostly boys, were forced on board the ship *Duty* and transported to Virginia.

From thence onward, English male child slaves came to be known as "Duty Boys" (Alexander Brown, *The First Republic in America,* p. 375). There would be many more shipments of these doomed children bound for the colonies in the years ahead.

"From that time on little is known about them except that very few lived to become adults. When a 'muster' or census of the (Virginia) colony was taken in 1625, the names of only seven boys were listed (of the children kidnapped in 1619). All the rest were dead... The statistics for the children sent in 1 620 are equally grim ...no more than five were alive in 1625." (Johnson, p. 147).

On April 30, 1621 Sir Edwin Sandys presented a plan to the English parliament for the solution of the threat poor English people posed to the fabulously wealthy aristocracy: mass shipment to Virginia, where they would all be "brought to goodness."

When control of the colony of Virginia passed from the privately-held Virginia Company directly to the king, it was deemed more expedient, as time went on, to privatize the traffic in White children while placing it on an even larger basis to meet the cheap labor needs of all the colonies. In this way the Crown avoided the opprobrium that might have been connected with the further official sale of English children even as the aristocracy covertly expanded this slave trade dramatically.

The early traffic in White children to Virginia had proved profitable not only for the Virginia Company but for the judges and other officials in England who administered the capture of the children:

J. Ferrar, treasurer of the Virginia Company, indicated that he had been approached by the Marshal of London and other officials who had been involved in procuring children for the colony, proclaiming that they were owed a financial reward "for their care and travail therein, that they might be encouraged hereafter to take the like pains whensoever they should have again the like occasion." The officials subsequently received the handsome "cut" for their part in the loathsome traffic in kidnapped White children which they had desired. (Susan M. Kingsbury, ed., *The Records of the Virginia Company of London,* vol. one, p. 424 and Johnson, pp. 144-145).

This collusion between the public and private sphere generated profits and established a precedent for many more "occasions" where "like pains" would be eagerly taken. The precedent established was the cornerstone of the trade in child-slaves in Britain for decades to come; a trade whose center, after London, would become the ports of Scotland:

"Press gangs in the hire of local merchants roamed the streets, seizing 'by force such boys as seemed proper subjects for the slave trade.' Children were driven in flocks through the town and confined for shipment in barns... So flagrant was the practice that people in the countryside about Aberdeen avoided bringing children into the city for fear they might be stolen; and so widespread was the collusion of merchants, shippers, suppliers and even magistrates that the man who exposed it was forced to recant and run out of town." (Van der Zee, *Bound Over,* p. 210).

This man was Peter Williamson who as a child in 1743 was captured in Aberdeen and sold as a slave to the *Planter*, a "White Guineaman." The *Planter* was destined for America with 70 other kidnapped Scottish children in addition to other freight. After eleven weeks at sea, the ship ran aground on a sand bar near Cape May on the Delaware river. As it began to take on water, the crew fled in a lifeboat, leaving the boys to drown in the sinking ship. The *Planter* managed to stay afloat until morning however, and the slavers returned to salvage their "cargo."

Peter Williamson was twice-blessed. He not only survived the *Planter* but had the great good fortune to have been purchased by a former slave, Hugh Wilson, who had also been kidnapped in Scotland as a child. Wilson had fled slavery in another colony and now bought Williamson in Pennsylvania. He did so solely out of compassion, knowing the boy would be bought by someone else had Wilson not bought him first. Wilson paid for Williamson's education in a colonial school and years later on his death, bequeathed to the lad his horse, saddle and a small sum of money, all Wilson had in the world.

With this advantage, Williamson married, became an Indian-fighter on the frontier and eventually made his way back to Scotland, seeking justice for himself and on behalf of all kidnapped children including his deceased friend Hugh Wilson. This took the form of a book, *The Life and Curious Adventures of Peter Williamson, Who Was Carried Off from Aberdeen and Sold for a Slave*.

But when he attempted to distribute it in Aberdeen he was arrested on a charge of publishing a "scurrilous and infamous libel, reflecting greatly upon the character and reputations of the merchants of Aberdeen." The book was ordered to be publicly burned and Williamson jailed. He was eventually fined and banished from the city.

Williamson did not give up but sued the judges of Aberdeen and took sworn statements from people who had witnessed kidnappings or who had had their own children snatched by slavers. Typical was the testimony of William Jamieson of Oldmeldrum, a farming village 1 2 miles from Aberdeen. In 1741, Jamieson's ten year old son John was captured by a "spirit" gang in the employ of "Bonny John" Burnet, a powerful slave-merchant based in Aberdeen.

After making inquiries, Jamieson learned that his son was being held for shipment to the "Plantations." Jamieson hurried to Aberdeen and frantically searched the docks and ships for his boy. He found him on shore among a circle of about sixty other boys, guarded by Bonny John's slavers who brandished horse whips. When the boys walked outside the circle they were whipped. Jamieson called to his son to come to him. The boy tried to run to his father. Father and son were beaten to the ground by the slavers.

Jamieson sought a writ from the Scottish courts but was informed "that it would be vain for him to apply to the magistrates to get his son liberate; because some of the magistrates had a hand in those doings." Jamieson never saw his son alive again, "having never heard of him since he was carried away."

The testimony from Jamieson and from many others helped Peter Williamson to prevail. The Aberdeen merchants were ordered by the Edinburgh Court of Sessions to pay him £100. Williamson was personally vindicated and his book was printed in a new edition. The kidnapping continued, however.

The enslavement of White children from Great Britain later became the subject of a much better known book, Robert Louis Stevenson's *Kidnapped*, which was based on the real-life case of

James Annesley whose uncle, the Earl of Anglesey, had arranged for him to be seized and sold into slavery in America, in order to remove any challenge to the Earl's inheritance of his brother's estates.

Annesley was savagely whipped and brutally mistreated in America and it appeared he would die in chains. He was eventually re-sold to another master who accepted his story that he was an English lord and the heir to the Anglesey barony.

Annesley managed to make his way back to Scotland where he wrote a book, *Memoirs of an Unfortunate Young Nobleman, Returned from Thirteen Years' Slavery in America,* which years later came to the attention of Robert Louis Stevenson. Unfortunately this rare case involving the enslavement of a member of the English nobility attracted attention only because it involved royalty. The far more common plight of hundreds of thousands of poor British children who had languished and died in slavery in the colonies was ignored and awareness of the history of their ordeal remained unchanged in the wake of the publication of Stevenson's classic.

The head of one kidnapping ring, John Stewart, sold at least 500 White youths per year into slavery in the colonies. Stewart's thugs were paid twenty-five shillings for Whites they procured by force— usually a knock in the head with a blunt instrument— or fraud. Stewart sold the Whites to the masters of the "White Guineaman" slave ships for forty shillings each.

One eyewitness to the mass kidnapping of poor Whites estimated that 10,000 were sold into slavery every year from throughout Great Britain (information in a pamphlet by M. Godwyn, London, 1680).

White Losses in the Middle Passage Higher than that of Blacks

White slaves transported to the colonies suffered a staggering loss of life in the 17th and 18th century. During the voyage to America it was customary to keep the White slaves below deck for the entire nine to twelve week journey. A White slave would be confined to a hole not more than sixteen feet long, chained with 50 other men to a board, with padlocked collars around their necks. The weeks of confinement below deck in the ship's stifling hold often resulted in outbreaks of contagious disease which would sweep through the "cargo" of White "freight" chained in the bowels of the ship.

Ships carrying White slaves to America often lost half their slaves to death. According to historian Sharon V. Salinger, "Scattered data reveal that the mortality for [White] servants at certain times equaled that for [Black] slaves in the 'middle passage,' and during other periods actually exceeded the death rate for [Black] slaves." (Salinger, p.91.) Salinger reports a death rate of ten to twenty percent over the entire 18th century for Black slaves on board ships enroute to America compared with a death rate of 25% for White slaves enroute to America (Salinger, p. 92).

Foster R. Dulles writing in *Labor in America: A History,* p. 6, states that whether convicts, children 'spirited' from the countryside or political prisoners, White slaves "experienced discomforts and sufferings on their voyage across the Atlantic that paralleled the cruel hardships undergone by negro slaves on the notorious Middle Passage."

Dulles says the Whites were "indiscriminately herded aboard the 'white guineamen,' often as many as 300 passengers on little vessels of not more than 200 tons burden— overcrowded, unsanitary... The mortality rate was sometimes as high as 50% and young children seldom survived the horrors of a voyage which might last anywhere from seven to twelve weeks."

Independent investigator A.B. Ellis in the *Argosy* writes concerning the transport of White slaves, "The human cargo, many of whom were still tormented by unhealed wounds, could not all lie down at once without lying on each other. They were never suffered to go on deck. The hatchway was constantly watched by sentinels armed with hangers and blunder busses. In the dungeons below all was darkness, stench, lamentation, disease and death."

Marcus Jernegan describes the greed of the shipmasters which led to horrendous loss of life for White slaves transported to America:

"The voyage over often repeated the horrors of the famous 'middle passage' of slavery fame. An average cargo was three hundred, but the shipmaster, for greater profit, would sometimes crowd as many as six hundred into a small vessel... The mortality under such circumstances was tremendous, sometimes more than half... Mittelberger (an eyewitness) says he saw thirty-two children thrown into the ocean during one voyage. (Jernegan, pp. 50-51).

"The mercantile firms, as importers of (White) servants, were not too careful about their treatment, as the more important purpose of the transaction was to get ships over to South Carolina which could carry local produce back to Europe. Consequently the Irish— as well as others— suffered greatly...

"It was almost as if the British merchants had redirected their vessels from the African coast to the Irish coast, with the white servants coming over in much the same fashion as the Arican slaves." (Warren B. Smith, p. 42).

A study of the middle passage of White slaves was included in Parliamentary Petition of 1659. It reported that White slaves were locked below deck for two weeks while the slaveship was still in port. Once under way, they were "all the way locked up under decks... amongst horses." They were chained from their legs to their necks.

"...transports... travel in double irons... were whipped and beaten... captains such as Edward Brockett of the *Rappahannock Merchant,* were totally unfit." (Ekirch, p. 101). Of the White slaves bound for Maryland from London aboard the slaveship *Justitia,* at the mercy of the savage Capt. Barnet Bond, nearly one-third of the Whites died: "The very worst excesses were revealed during the voyage of the *Justitia* in 1743. Under the command of Barnet Bond... Bond set stringent water rations. Despite ample reserves of water on board, he allotted each transport only one pint a day. Some started to drink their own urine..." (Ekirch, p. 102).

The former partner of Andrew Reid of the White slave trading firm of Reid & Armour wrote that Reid was "a person against whom every species of complaint was made." Profits continued to flow in spite of the deaths of what the White slave-trade firm of Stevenson, Randolph & Cheston referred to as "the goods." The traffic in these "goods... properly managed will in a few years make us very genteel fortunes. The sales of the convicts run up amazingly in a little time." (William Stevenson to James Cheston, Sept. 12,

1768 and Dec. 30, 1769, *Cheston-Galloway Papers,* Maryland Historical Society).

Once the slaveships left British shores, "profit rather than penal policy shaped the character of transportation" and what happened to enslaved Whites overseas "mattered little. As soon as they were safely consigned to merchants, authorities assumed no responsibility for their welfare." (Ekirch, p. 3). White slaves aboard ship were treated "worse than dogs or swine and are kept much more uncleanly than those animals are..." (Shaw, p. 35).

A witness who saw a White slave aboard a ship owned by the slaver John Stewart, reported: "All the states of horror I ever had an idea of are much short of what I saw this man in; chained to a board in a hole not above sixteen feet long, more than fifty with him; a collar and padlock about his neck, and chained to five of the most dreadful creatures I ever looked on." Another observer watching the auction of a hundred White slaves in Williamsburg, Virginia remarked, "I never seen such passels of poor wretches in my life. Some almost naked..." (Ekirch, pp. 100 and 122).

One White woman slave bound for Australia, Elizabeth Dudgeon, had dared to talk back to a guard. She was trussed up to a ship's grating and mercilessly whipped. One of the ship's officers relished watching her lashed: "The corporal did not play with her, but laid it home, which I was very glad to see... she has long been fishing for it, which she has at last got to her heart's content." (*Journal of Ralph Clark,* entry of July 3, 1787).

In order to realize the maximum profit from the trade in White slaves, the captains of the White Guineamen crammed their ships with as many poor Whites as possible, certain that even with the most callous disregard for the lives of the Whites the financial gain would still make the trip worth the effort. A loss of 20% of their White "cargo" was regarded as acceptable. But sometimes losses were much higher.

Out of 350 White slaves on a ship bound for the colonies in 1638 only 80 arrived alive. "We have thrown over board two and three in a day for many dayes together" wrote Thomas Rous, a survivor of the trip. A ship carrying White slaves in 1685, the *Betty of London,* left England with 100 White slaves and arrived in the colonies with 49 left.

A number of factors contributed to the higher death rates for White slaves than Blacks. Although the goal of maximum profits motivated both trades, it cost more to obtain Blacks from Africa than it did to capture Whites in Europe. White slaves were not cared for as well as Blacks because the Whites were cheaply obtained and were viewed as expendable.

"The African slave trade was not fully established in the early 17th century... The price of African slaves was prohibitively high and the English were neither familiar with nor committed to black slavery as a basic institution" (Beckles, *White Servitude,* p. 3).

Ship Captains involved in the White slave trade obtained White slaves with penal status either free of charge or were subsidized to take them, and for all other categories of White slaves, they paid at most a small sum to an agent to procure them, forfeiting only the cost of their keep on board ship if they died.[6]

---

[6] "The greater part of the convict trade was concentrated in the hands of a few merchant companies... In London, which offered the special lure of the Treasury subsidy, several firms captured the market for the bulk of the century... Andrew Reid, a friend of the Secretary of the Treasury, was placed on the government's payroll... Reid had several partners, including James and Andrew Armour of London and John Stewart, a Scotsman. During the 1750s, Stewart and the Armours held the Treasury contract. Thereafter Stewart was joined by fellow Scot Duncan Campbell.. Other London merchants, though not

Moreover, traders in Black slaves operated ships designed solely for the purpose of carrying human cargo with the intent of creating conditions whereby as many Black slaves as possible would reach America alive. White slave ships were cargo ships with no special provisions for passengers.

In addition, transportation rules decreed that, in cases where White slaves were sold in advance to individual planters in America, if the White slave survived the voyage beyond the halfway point in the journey, the planter in America— not the captain of the slave ship— would be responsible for the costs of the White slaves' provisions whether or not the slave survived the trip. Captains of the slaveships became infamous for providing sufficient food for only the first half of the trip and then virtually starving their White captives until they arrived in America.

"Jammed into filthy holds, manacled, starved and abused, they suffered and died during the crossings in gross numbers. Thousands were children under 12, snatched off the streets..." (Kendall, p. 1).

"...the transportation ...became a profitable enterprise. Traders delivered thousands of bound laborers to Pennsylvania and exhibited a callous disregard for their... cargoes" (Salinger, p. 88). As a result, White slaves on board these ships suffered a high rate of disease. "...transportation (of White slaves) remained a branch of commerce wedded to carrying human cargoes at minimal expense... sizable numbers never reached American shores... from disease, mistreatment... (Ekirch, p. 108).

---

government beneficiaries, trafficked in convicts on a smaller scale. There (were) thirty-four identifiable London firms involved in the trade to Maryland from 1746 to 1775..." [Ekirch, pp. 73-74].

The number of diseased White slaves arriving was high enough for Pennsylvania officials to recommend a quarantine law for them. Thus a new torment was to be endured for White slaves who "were often stopped just short of the New World, with land in sight, and forced to remain quarantined on board ships in which they had just spent a horrifying ten to twelve weeks" (Salinger, p. 89).

In 1738 Dr. Thomas Graeme reported to the colonial Council of Pennsylvania that if two ships crammed with White slaves were allowed to land, "it might prove Dangerous to the health of the Inhabitants of this Province." ("Minutes of the Provincial Council of Pennsylvania," *Colonial Records,* 4:306).

Ships filled with diseased White slaves landed anyway. In 1750 an island was established for their quarantine, Fisher Island, at the mouth of Schuylkill River. But the establishment of the quarantine area did nothing to protect the health of the White slaves and the island was more typical of Devil's Island than a place of recuperation. In 1764 a clergyman, Pastor Helmuth, visited Fisher island and described it as "a land of the living dead, a vault full of living corpses."

White Slaves Treated Worse than Blacks

"Before 1650, however, the greater victims of man's inhumanity were the mass of white Christian servants who suffered at the hands of callous, white Christian masters. For the time being, with all of their troubles, the blacks had it better." (Bridenbaugh, p. 120).

"Sold to a master in Merion, near Philadelphia, David Evans was put to work 'hewing and uprooting trees'— land clearing, the most arduous of colonial labor, work that was spared black slaves because they were too valuable." (Van der Zee, p. 138).

"Negroes... are, therefore, almost in every instance, under ore comfortable circumstances than the miserable European, over whom the rigid planter exercises an inflexible rigidity. They are strained to the utmost to perform their allotted labor... they frequently try to escape, but very few are successful... and... when apprehended, are committed to close confinement, advertised, and delivered to their respective masters... The unhappy culprit is doomed to a severe chastisement; and a prolongation of servitude is decreed... Those who survive... seldom establish their residence..." (William Eddis, *Letters From America,* [published in 1792] Letter VI).

In the British West Indies the torture visited upon White slaves by their masters was routine. Masters hung White slaves by their hands and set their hands afire as a means of punishment. To end this barbarity, Colonel William Brayne wrote to English authorities in 1656 urging the importation of negro slaves on the grounds that, "as the planters would have to pay much for them, they would have an interest in preserving their lives, which was wanting in the case of (Whites)..." many of whom, he charged, were killed by overwork and cruel treatment.

Indentures: An Organized Racket

Even privileged 17th and 18th century "apprentices" often became slaves in the end (i.e. unpaid, forced laborers for life) based on contractual trickery, judicial malfeasance and usury employed against them during their supposedly limited term as indentured servants.

Such an apprentice would be enticed to borrow sums of money, sign a contract with impossible provisions guaranteeing his or her violation of the contractual terms and other unscrupulous means of extending both the period of servitude as well as broadening the scope of the servant's obligations. By these means an apprentice could be transformed into a slave for life.

Free White people were sometimes induced to sign "indentures" and place themselves in voluntary "temporary" slavery with the promise of obtaining farm acreage at the end of their term of indenture. An American colony typically offered 50 acres to such persons.

This was actually little more than an organized racket. The alleged "servant" had his or her land grant entrusted to the landowner for whom they labored, with the understanding that title would pass to the servant at the end of his term of labor. But he could forfeit his rights to this promised land on the slightest pretext of his owner, on such grounds as running away (the owner's word would do) or for "indolence."

For the price of a White slave's transport— six pounds— his owner secured a "headright" to the land which was supposedly intended to go to the "servant" but which was instead combined with the land supposedly set aside for other White slaves and formed into an estate which would multiply in value. By this means and with an occasional additional fee to an English merchant or "spirit" who provided the landowner with kidnapped extra White slaves, the plantation owners of colonial America played Monopoly with the fertile valleys and wooded uplands of Maryland and Virginia. Meanwhile the rightful owners of this land lay in paupers' graves or enshackled for life. This monopolistic grip on the land market was detrimental to all White laborers.

Those White slaves who did manage to obtain their freedom after thirty or forty years as chattel, were swindled out of the spectral "freedom dues" of acreage, left to exist as landless peasants and scorned as "hillbillies" and "White trash," in spite of decades of labor under monstrous conditions of hardship.

"One would like to think that some of the few survivors went on to become prominent leaders of the colony or were the founders of great families. This does not appear to be the case... Some were doubtless the progenitors of the 'poor white trash' of the South... many of the free whites who had descended from the poorer elements of the white servant class became objects of charity... (Johnson, p. 147; Jernegan, pp. 56 and 178).

"...at no time after 1640 in either Barbados or St. Christopher, and probably Nevis, was there any cheap land enough for a man to purchase with his freedom dues... the vast majority never became landholders..." (Bridenbaugh, p. 113).

"It then became the custom to give the servant at the end of his term, not land, but three hundred pounds of sugar, worth less than two pounds sterling... It was hardly worth the servant's while to endure the conditions which have been described for... ($4 worth) of sugar." (Eric Williams, pp. 102-103).

Freed White slaves "experienced hard times." In a study of 145 White freedmen residing in Kent County, Maryland, "only five could be traced with reasonable certainty in property records for all of Maryland, including wills, estate inventories and debt books which were compilations of landholdings." And among the five former White slaves who did leave an inventory of their goods, "none was well-to do."

"A study of All Hallow's Parish, Maryland has shown that whereas one-third of adult White males did not own land around 1700, nearly half were non-landowners by the middle of the century ...In the mid-18th century, newly freed servants trying to enter the ranks of small planters encountered severe obstacles. Besides lacking capital to buy tools, seed, livestock... few of them could afford the land... in Virginia large numbers never received freedom dues..."

Moreover, "Years of servitude so ruined the health" of some former White slaves, "that no one would hire them" once they were free. (Ekirch, pp. 179, 180, 182-183). In fact some White slaves, out of extreme poverty, signed new contracts of indenture, contributing to a pattern of life-long servitude.

These White former slaves' share of the accumulated wealth of the American colonies, measured by any standard, was negligible; their say in the planter aristocracy was virtually non-existent. They were the "expendable" by-products and survivors of a system of exploitation governed solely by merchant companies chartered in England by aristocratic fiat. It was the exclusive government by a merchant company which Adam Smith assailed as the worst of all governments for any country.

Often working conditions were made especially gruesome toward the end of the period when the servant's contract was due to expire in order to induce him to run away, lose his 50 acres and be held extra years in enslavement for fleeing. "Toward the end of the term of servitude, working conditions would often be deliberately worsened, tempting the man to run away so the master might gain these advantages" (Kendall, p.7).

Of 5,000 "indentured servants" who entered the colony of Maryland between 1670 and 1680, fewer than 1300 proved their rights to their 50 acre "freedom dues." What had become of the others? More than 1400 died from overwork, chronic malnourishment and disease. The others were defrauded.

"By the 18th century the white servant class was disillusioned... The planters had... squashed the laboring Whites... They were the easy pawns of the planters, who despised them..." (Beckles, "Rebels and Reactionaries," pp. 18-19).

The statutes overseeing non-penal indentured servitude in colonial America were mere windowdressing and neither these statutes or the Common Law proved any obstacle to the gradual enslavement of those with the non-penal status of "indentured servant," by means of tacking on extra time to be served, on the basis of fabricated or trumped charges and minor offenses.

A Virginia law of 1619 provided that "if a servant willfully neglect his master's commands he shall suffer bodily punishment." When Wyatt became Governor in 1621 he was ordered to see that punishment for offenses committed by White slaves would also be in terms of labor on behalf of the colonial government, such labor to be performed after the slave fulfilled his original period of service to his master. This is the evil practice of lengthening the time required for the White person's term of labor, a practice which quickly resulted in the lengthening of the term of "service" by years and ended in the perpetual enslavement of the White.

"While it is true that the Common Law of England had the status of national law with territorial extent in the colonies, the relation of Master to servant in cases of what began as non-penal indentured servitude, was unknown to the Common Law and could neither be derived from nor regulated by it" (cf. Richard B. Morris, "Massachusetts and the Common Law," *American History Review,* 1926).

Both indentured servitude and the White slavery permitted under the rubric of the penal codes, depended for their regulation and sanction on special local statutes and tribunals which acted as the "necessities of the occasion" demanded.

The legacy of White enslavement bound up in the medieval English legal concept of "villeinage" contributed an informal framework or milieu at least, for legitimizing the enslavement of the White poor in British-America. In this light, Richard B. Morris is only partially correct. There was in fact precedent for White slavery in Common Law but it was little cited in the colonies, perhaps because such formal legal citation would have exposed the indentures racket for what it was. (5)

Biblical provisions for bound and hired labor were cited to justify White slavery in early America, on the grounds that it was Scriptural and therefore humane. The Body of Liberties of 1641, the first law code of Puritan New England, established four categories of servitude, citing Exodus 21:2; Leviticus 25:39-55 and Deuteronomy 23:15-16. However, had those Scriptures actually been obeyed, the enslavement of Christians (the heirs of the Israelites), would never have taken place.

Deuteronomy mandates that a bondsman is not to be oppressed. Exodus decrees that the term of service will under no circumstance exceed six years. Leviticus forbids forced slavery for the payment of debts as well as child slavery (cf. 25: 40-41). The permanent enslavement of racial aliens and their children *was permitted* (Leviticus 25:45-46, Exodus 21:4, which destroys the whole basis of Abraham Lincoln's Second Inaugural Address). (6)

Then as now, religious hypocrites of "Churchianity," as it more properly may be called, ignored Bible teachings on the subject even as they cited them for purposes of their own justification in enslaving fellow White Christians for pecuniary gain. (It should be noted that some individual masters in early America who felt convicted by the Scriptures regulating bonded kinsmen, moderated their treatment of White bondsmen accordingly).

In colonial America, White people could be enslaved for such an "offense" as missing church services more than three times or for "prevention of an idle course of life." In 1640 a Virginia master needed to ensure further labor from his White servants in order to place his investments and land improvements on a more secure basis. He therefore falsely accused a number of his servants of a conspiracy "to run out of the colony and enticing divers others to be actors in the same conspiracy." As a result of his accusation the alleged "runaways" were severely whipped and had their term of forced labor lengthened an additional seven years, to be served "in irons."

This can be regarded as a light sentence in view of the fact that seven years was a standard addition of the term of labor for the crime of running away, or conspiring to do so, to which would then be added, in terms of additional time, the expenses incurred for capture and return of the White to his master, such costs being likely to include rewards, sheriffs and slave-hunters' bounties and jail fees.

These latter were not fixed by law until 1726 and were a source of tremendous abuse by tacking on huge costs to the capture of the runaway and then commanding that the runaway pay for these inflated costs in terms of years of his life in further forced-labor.

A White slave who fled or was accused of fleeing often had his term of labor extended seven, ten or even fifteen years, as a result. White slave Lawrence Finny received an additional seven years, eleven months of forced labor for running away, while escaped White slave William Fisher on being caught, received an additional term of six years and 250 days (Petitions, Chester County, Pennsylvania, Court of Quarter Sessions, Aug. 1731 and June, 1732). Just for being absent from the plantation at any time, a White slave would be forced to undergo one additional year of slavery for every two hours he was absent. (Beckles, *White Servitude,* p. 84).

Starving White slaves who took extra food from their masters' overflowing larders were enslaved another two years for each commission of that "crime."

Punishment of Runaway White Slaves— Virginia, 1643: "Whereas, there are divers loitering runaways in the colony who very often absent themselves from their master's service... be it therefore enacted and confirmed, that all runaways that shall absent themselves from their said masters' service shall be liable to make satisfaction by service at the end of their time of indenture (viz.) double the time of service so neglected, *and in some cases more, if the commissioners for the place find it requisite and convenient...*" (Hening's Statutes at Large, vol. 1, 254 and 255, emphasis supplied).

Further accusations, infractions and violations added to these additions and in sum amounted to a lifetime of total enslavement and not the allegedly limited, benign White "indentured servitude" the professorcrats fleetingly refer to on their way to their semester-long devotion to negro slave studies.

Indeed, one-half of White "indentured servants" did not live to attain their freedom. Should anyone think this grim datum refers mainly to Whites enslaved in old age, it actually refers to Whites who were first "indentured" between the ages of 16 and 20. (Bridenbaugh, p. 123).

"The truth is," wrote White slave Edward Hill, "we live in the fearfullest age that ever Christians lived in."

Enslavement of the White Family

Young White females in bondage were denied the right to marry, a clever device for helping extend their servitude into full-fledged slavery since the penalty for a woman having a baby out of wedlock while a slave, was an extension of her term of slave labor another two and a half years. A White male slave had at least four years added to his time for having sex with a White female slave or for entering into a compact of marriage with her.

Twenty-three year old Henry Carman, a White slave since he had been kidnapped in London at the age of seventeen, made White slave Alice Chambers pregnant and received an additional seven years slavery for this "crime." (Johnson, p. 148).

A Virginia law of 1672 recognized that there were masters who had lengthened the enslavement of their White female slaves by making them pregnant by the slavemaster himself. No punishment was given to the master for such acts, however.

As bad as this may seem it cannot compare with the dreadful fate that awaited the children of the enslaved White mother. The "bastard" or "obscene" children, as they were called, of unmarried White women-slaves were bound over to the mother's slavemaster for a period of thirty-one years! This heinous child-slavery from birth was not modified until 1765 when the Assembly of Virginia declared it to be "an unreasonable severity to such children" and limited the term of bondage for such White children to a "mere" 21 years for boys and 18 years for girls.

This enslavement of White children in colonial America was based on the rule of the ancient Roman slave code which decreed, "Partus sequitur ventrem," (the condition of the child follows the condition of the mother) and which was assimilated by English legal scholars and applied in the colonies.

The following is an entry describing one such case of infant-enslavement:

"Margaret Micabin servant to Mr. David Crawley having a bastard Child, Mr. Crawley prays the gentlemen of this Vestry to bind out the said Child as they think fitt. It is ordered by the Vestry that the Church-Wardens bind out the said Child named John Sadler born the 26th July last 1720. The foresaid child is by indenture bound unto Mr. David Crawley to serve according to Law." (*The Vestry Book and Register of Bristol Parish Virginia, 1720-1789*).

At other times the baby was forcibly separated from the White slave mother shortly after birth. White woman Sally Brant was enslaved to the wealthy Quaker family of Henry and Elizabeth Drinker. Quakers were strong campaigners against negro slavery but some had few qualms about White slavery.

When Sally Brant's baby was born in the Drinker's country house, Sally was forced by the Drinkers to return to their main house in Philadelphia, leaving the newborn infant behind with a stranger. The White slave father of the child was also not allowed to see his baby and the infant subsequently died. Elizabeth Drinker, the wealthy Quaker slaveowner, kept a diary in which she philosophically noted that the death of her White slave's baby had most likely worked out for the best.

"Unmarried (White) women servants who became pregnant, as did an estimated 20 percent, received special punishment. All had to serve additional years; some had their children taken from them and sold, for a few pounds of tobacco, to another master." (Levine, p. 52).

By 1769 all children born to even free White women who were unmarried were also candidates for enslavement: "...in 1769... the church wardens were instructed to bind out illegitimate children of free single white women." (Jernegan, p. 180).

When Hell was in Session

Long hours and exposure to disease and the elements were considered part of a first year "seasoning" process it was thought a good White slave would require. A White slave would work from sunrise to sunset in the fields and then might be be put to work in a shed grinding corn until midnight or one a.m. and expected to return to the fields the next day at dawn. In some southern colonies with extreme heat, as many as 80% of a shipment of White slaves died in their first year in the New World.

Richard Ligon, a traveling writer and eyewitness to White slavery has written that he saw a White slave beaten with a cane, "about the head till the blood has followed for a fault that is not worth speaking of; and yet he must be patient, or worse will follow" (Ligon, p. 44). How many White tourists today who take winter vacations in such Caribbean islands as Jamaica and Barbados know that they are visiting the site of a gruesome holocaust against poor White people who died by the tens of thousands and were slaves in those islands long before Blacks ever were?

Historian Richard Dunn has stated that the early sugar plantations of the British West Indies were nothing more than mass graves for White workers (*Sugar and Slaves: The Rise of the Planter Class in the English West Indies,* p. 302). Four-fifths of the White slaves sent to the West Indies didn't survive the first year (Van der Zee, p. 183).

In 1688 a member of the nobility wrote from a British colony in the Caribbean islands to the British government, "I beg... care for the poor White servants here, who are used with more barbarous cruelty than if in Algiers. Their bodies and souls are used as if hell commenced here and only continued in the world to come." (Sir Thomas Montgomery to the Lords of Trade and Plantations, Aug. 3, 1688, *Calendar of State Papers, Colonial Series,* 1685-1688, p. 577).

"Twenty or more (White) servants laboring under the supervision of an overseer led the most wearisome and miserable lives... If a servant complained, the overseer would beat him; if he resisted, the master might double his time in bondage... the overseers act like those in charge of galley slaves... The cost in (White) lives of such inhuman treatment is incalculable, but it was very, very high." (Bridenbaugh, p. 107; Pere Biet, *Voyage,* p. 290)

One example of the horrible conditions under which White slaves labored can be glimpsed in the case of the White slave known to history as Boulton. In 1646 Boulton's master was suspected of cheating a colonial official of a large shipment of cotton. The master asked the White slave if he would take the blame. If Boulton made the bogus confession in place of his master he was liable to have both his ears cut off by the colonial officials as well as having more time added to his period of bondage.

However Boulton's master promised that he would not only ignore the extra time if Boulton agreed to take the blame for him, but that he would free Boulton from slavery after Boulton had been punished by the authorities. So desperate was Boulton to be free that Boulton agreed to pretend that his master had told him to give the cotton to the officials, but that instead he had embezzled it for his own use. Both of the White slave's ears were subsequently cut off. Afterward, his master kept his part of the bargain and Boulton was emancipated.

"Some planters grew so desperate for help that they would ransom white captives from the Indians, returning them to a servitude which, according to one complainant, 'differeth not from her slavery with the Indians.'" (Van der Zee, p. 85).

The Fugitive Slave Law: Escaping Whites Hunted and Tortured

"Fugitive Slave" laws, enacted to facilitate the apprehension and punishment of runaway White slaves is another suppressed aspect of the history of early America. William Hening in his 13 volume *Statutes at Large of Virginia* records that the punishment for runaway Whites was to be "branded in the cheek with the letter R." They also often had one or both of their ears cuts off.

In 1640 the General Court of Virginia ruled that two White slaves, "principall actors and contrivers in a most dangerous conspiracy by attempting to run out of the country and (by) Inticing divers others to be actors in said Conspiracy," be whipped, branded and required to serve the colony an additional seven years in leg irons.

In the stock scenes from Hollywood films like *Glory* the negro slave's shirt is dramatically lifted to reveal a back full of hideous scars from repeated whippings. This brings tears to the eyes of one of his White New England commanders in the fictional film *Glory*. Yet in reality, among the White soldiers in that scene there would have been more than a few who also bore massive scars from a whip or who had seen the scars of the lash on their White fathers' backs. The current image of Blacks as predominantly the ones who bore the scars of the whiplash is in error.

On Sept. 20, 1776 the Continental Congress authorized the whipping of unruly American enlisted men with up to one hundred lashes. There are cases on record of rank and file White American troops receiving up to two hundred-fifty whip-lashes! (Walter J. Fraser, Jr., "Reflections of 'Democracy' in Revolutionary South Carolina," in *The Southern Common People,* p.16).

This incredible savagery represented the level of treatment poor Whites sometimes experienced at the hands of the authorities in 18th century America "...the officer class... came to use the lash unsparingly (on)... unpropertied... recruits... the poor white rank and file..." (Fraser, p. 17).

Savage whippings of White Americans also occurred in the U.S. Navy in the 19th century. An eyewitness to Black slavery in the South and the treatment of White sailors on American naval ships at sea reported, "...that on board of the American man-of-war that carried him out... he had witnessed more flogging than had taken place on... (a) plantation of five hundred African slaves in ten years." (Herman Melville, *White Jacket or The World in a Man of War,* Oxford University Press edition, p. 142).[7]

A decade before Melville's account was published, Richard Henry Dana's *Two Years Before the Mast* appeared. The author, a Harvard law student who had signed on a ship to test his manhood, gave the following account of the whipping of a White sailor:

"Can't a man ask a question without being flogged?'

"No,' shouted the captain; 'nobody shall open his mouth aboard this vessel but myself;' and began laying the blows upon his

---

[7] Melville was an experienced sailor from the age of nineteen. He wrote *White Jacket* based on his fourteen month voyage aboard the Navy frigate United States, during which he witnessed 163 floggings of sailors.

back, swinging half round between each blow to give it full effect. As he went on his passion increased, and he danced about the deck, calling out as he swung the rope, 'if you want to know what I flog you for, I'll tell you. It's because I like to do it! It suits me! That's what I do it for!'

"The man writhed under the pain, until he could endure it no longer, when he called out... 'Oh, Jesus Christ! Oh, Jesus Christ!'

"Don't call on Jesus Christ,' shouted the captain; *'he can't help you. Call on Captain T—* he's the man. He can help you. Jesus Christ can't help you now!... You see your condition! You see where I've got you all, and you know what to expect!... I'll flog you all, fore and aft, from the (cabin) boy up!"

In White Jacket, Melville describes the whipping of a teenage sailor named Peter who had defended himself against an attack by a bully, rather than report the attack to the ship's captain. For this he was ordered stripped and "scourged worse than a hound":

"As he was being secured to the gratings, and the shudderings and creepings of his dazzlingly white back were revealed, he turned round his head imploringly; but his weeping entreaties and vows of contrition were of no avail. 'I would not forgive God Almighty!' cried the captain.

"The fourth boatswain's mate advanced, and at the first blow, the boy, shouting 'My God! Oh my God!' writhed and leaped so as to displace the gratings, and scatter the nine tails of the scourge all over his person. At the next blow he howled, leaped and raged in unendurable torture." (Melville, *White Jacket,* p. 139).

There was a special class of whipping, "known in the navy as flogging through the fleet... this law may be and has been, quoted in judicial justification of the infliction of more than one hundred lashes... a sailor, under the above article, may legally be flogged to death.

To say, that after being flogged through the fleet, the prisoner's back is sometimes puffed up like a pillow; or to say that in other cases it looks as if burned black before a roasting fire; or to say that you may track him through the squadron by the blood on the bulwarks of every ship, would only be saying what many seamen have seen... Instances have occurred where he has expired the day after the punishment." (Melville, *White Jacket,* pp. 373-375).

When negro slaves were whipped in America it became a *cause celebré* for "humanitarians" throughout the West, continually cited, immortalized and lamented from that day to our own.

On the few occasions when the record of merciless whippings of White people has received an airing, Establishment historians insist that it be placed "in context":

"Flogging (of White sailors) was common, but it must be remembered that this was a harsh age, and it is absurd to judge it nearly two centuries later by modern humanitarian standards." (Dudley Pope, *The Devil Himself: The Mutiny of 1800,* p. xiv).

White slaves "found themselves powerless as individuals, without honor or respect, and driven into commodity production not by any inner sense of moral duty but by the outer stimulus of the whip." (Beckles, *White Servitude,* p. 5).

"In 1744 provision was made for whipping escaped servants through the parish, after proof had been made before a justice of the peace that they were fugitives...

"Dennis Mahoon was sentenced to be stripped naked to his waist and receive thirty-nine lashes upon his naked back.' This was his punishment for a second offense in persuading fellow servants to run away..." (Warren B. Smith, p. 76).

"(White) servants were tortured for confessions (fire was inserted between their fingers and knotted ropes were put about their necks)..." (Beckles, "Rebels and Reactionaries," p. 14).

"Taking flight was an act of resistance that required uncommon boldness. In addition to the dangers of the wilds, runaways risked severe penalties if they were caught.

"As in the case of fugitive (Black) slaves, these included a stiff whipping and being forced to wear a heavy iron collar called a 'pot-hook' around the neck." (Ekirch, p. 196).

Not only White slaves were brutalized but also those who dared to aid them in gaining their freedom.

The image of fugitive White slaves being hunted, whipped and jailed and the same treatment being accorded those who assisted fellow Whites out of slavery, is completely absent from modern textbook accounts of American history.

Yet even as late as the mid-18th century, of 1,724 wanted notices for fugitives from servitude, "the great majority" were White "indentured servants" (Jonathan Prude, "Runaway Ads and the Appearance of Unfree Laborers in America, 1750-1800," *The Journal of American History,* June, 1991, p. 139).[8]

Those who helped White slaves run away in colonial America were known as "enticers" and received 30 lashes with a whip if caught. Merely to counsel a White slave to seek his freedom was

---

[8] Some researchers, while hesitant to describe White slaves for what they were, are no longer content to describe servile Whites as "indentured," preferring such constructions as "unfree" and "bound laborer." The term "indentured servant" is meaningless as a racially distinct category of bondage since plenty of Blacks were "indentured" for a temporary term of service after which they became free persons who sometimes owned slaves themselves (J.H. Brewer, "Negro Property Owners in 17th Century Virginia." *Wm. and Mary Quarterly,* Oct. 1955).

considered by the colonial courts as illegal interference with the property rights of the rich and resulted in criminal penalties.

Hening states that to reduce the number of runaway White slaves a pass was required for any person leaving the Virginia colony and masters of ships were put under severe penalty for taking any White slave to freedom.

For a majority of the White slaves who ran away, "compatriots provided practical assistance and moral support. William Neilson, for instance, the 'ringleader' and spokesman for several Scottish runaways, was literate enough to forge passes for the entire band... in 1 745 two runaways from Caroline County, Virginia were reportedly concealed in Norfolk by a 'lame shoemaker...'" (Ekirch, pp. 198, 202).

Notices of runaway White slaves in South Carolina newspapers included specific warnings against harboring or assisting the fugitive White slaves and listed the statutory criminal penalties for doing so.

Certificates of freedom were required to be carried on the person of freed White slaves at all times. All White workers and poor in colonial America were regarded as suspect— guilty of being fugitive slaves unless they could "give an intelligent account of themselves" or show their certificate; a very convenient arrangement for enslaving free White men and women in America by claiming they were fugitive White slaves.

White slaves who ran away found safe haven in portions of North Carolina which became known in Virginia as the "Refuge of Runaways." The mountains of Appalachia also served as hideouts for fugitive White slaves. The hunting of White slaves became a lucrative practice. In Virginia in 1699 persons who successfully hunted a White slave received 1,000 lbs. of tobacco, paid for by the future labor that would be extracted from the White slave.

In the 18th century many runaway White slaves headed for crowded cities like Philadelphia and New York that offered anonymity, "in which places no questions are asked," as one White runaway put it. Taverns in northern colonial cities were famous as places that concealed fugitive White slaves. (John K. Alexander, *Render Them Submissive: Responses to Poverty in Philadelphia, 1760-1800*, p. 62; Douglas Greenberg, Crime and Law Enforcement in the Colony of New York, pp. 97 and 198).

Richard B. Morris describes the appearance of fugitive White slaves: "One culprit was described as having a string of bells (fastened) around his neck which made a hideous jingling and discordant noise, another wore an iron collar, and others bore the scars of recent whippings on their backs" (Morris, *Government and Labor in Early America*, p. 435).

Advertisements regularly appeared in early American newspapers for fugitive White slaves. One such wanted notice described a slave who had run off as having a "long visage of lightish complexion, and thin-flaxen hair; sometimes ties his hair behind with a string, a very proud fellow... very impudent..." (Jernegan, p. 52).

"Physical descriptions printed in provincial newspaper advertisements for runaway servants provide an invaluable profile... Bent backs, ugly burns, and crooked limbs reflected the common hardships... Scars criss-crossed entire bodies... knife and sword wounds were common over all parts of the body... Among injuries received during servitude were marks left by whips, chains and iron collars. Thomas Burns, for example, was 'remarkably cut on the buttocks by a flogging' from his master, whereas Sarah Davis's whipping had left 'many scars on her back." (Ekirch, pp. 157-159).

The history of "racist White toleration" of the hunting of negro slaves as well as the controversy surrounding the capture of fugitive Black slaves in the North just prior to the Civil War is incomprehensible without being placed in the context of the body of Fugitive Slave Law that was first established for use against White slaves. In colonial America the fugitive White slave was considered the property of the master and the legal right to recovery was universally recognized.

The Articles of the New England Confederation provided that where a White slave fled his master for another colony in the Confederation, upon certification by one judge in the colony to which the White slave had fled, the fugitive would be delivered back into slavery.

Classed with "thieves and other criminals," the fugitive White slave could be pursued "by hue and cry" on land and over water, and men and boats were often impressed in the hunt for him. Magistrates, sheriffs or constables were authorized by statute to whip the fugitive White man severely before returning him to his master— twenty to thirty-nine lashes being the usual sentence imposed.

Massachusetts authorized that any White slave who had been previously whipped for running away was to be whipped again just for being found outside his master's farm without a note of permission from the slavemaster.

Between February 12, 1732 and December 20, 1735, the *South Carolina Gazette* carried 110 wanted notices for fugitive Black slaves and forty-one notices for fugitive White slaves.

The claims of masters in one colony upon the fugitive White slaves in another jurisdiction were allowed from the beginning of colonial settlement in America. The U.S. Constitution upheld the colonial fugitive White slave laws in its Article IV, section 2:

"No person held to service or labor in one state, under the Laws thereof escaping into another, shall, in Consequence of any Law or Regulation therein, be discharged from such Service or Labor, but shall be delivered up on a claim of the Party to whom such Service or Labor may be due."

This law was enacted by Whites against fellow White people and allowed White slavery to continue in some parts of America right up until the Civil War. The first legal blow to the system of White bondage didn't occur until 1821 when an Indiana court began to enforce the Ordinance of 1787 prohibiting White slavery in the old "Northwest Territory." The decision cited the Constitution of the state of Indiana which in turn drew its base from the 1 787 Ordinance in holding all White slavery null, void and unenforceable. The Thirteenth Amendment to the Constitution dealt a fatal blow to White slavery.

The enslavement of Whites in one form or another has proved very durable. Bound White servitude for orphans and destitute children on contracts of indenture still occurred in New York state as recently as 1923.

White Slaves in the American Revolution

During the American Revolution the Continental Congress, desperate for fighting manpower, permitted the recruitment of White slaves into the army, which was tantamount to granting them their freedom. This was not particularly radical however, in view of the fact that "four score and seven years" before Lincoln's Emancipation Proclamation, Lord Dunmore, the Royal Governor of Virginia, freed the negroes in his jurisdiction in the hope they would join the "Ethiopian Regiment" he had formed and fight the patriots (Ronald Hoffman, pp. 281-282).

In 1765, a fourteen year old Irish lad, Matthew Lyon, was orphaned when his father was executed along with other leaders of the "White Boys," an Irish farmer's association organized to resist British government confiscation of their farmlands. The boy was enslaved and transported to America where he was purchased by a wealthy Connecticut merchant.[9]

Later he was made to endure the shame of being sold to another master in exchange for two deer "which was a source of no

---

[9] "...the (Irish) peasant resorted to violence in self-protection, to resist the sometimes impossible demands of (the) landlord... to keep his miserable little plot of land— his only safeguard against starvation... The White-Boy Associations were in a sense, a 'vast trades union for the protection of the Irish peasantry...'" (Shaw, pp. 172-174).

end of scoffs and jeers" at Lyon's "irreparable disgrace of being sold for a pair of stags." (Pliny H. White, *Life and Services of Matthew Lyon,* p. 6)

By the spring of 1775 Matthew Lyon had taken advantage of the manpower shortage of the American Revolution and joined an obscure, rag-tag band of guerrilla fighters. Lyon and his fellow rebels were destined to enter the annals of historical fame when not long afterward they appeared out of nowhere at Ticonderoga in northern New York where their commander, Ethan Allen, demanded the surrender of the mighty British fort. Matthew Lyon had joined the Green Mountain Boys.

"Eighty five of us," Lyon would later recall with pride, "took from one hundred and forty British veterans the Fort Ticonderoga." The guns, cannon and ammunition obtained at Ticonderoga would supply the American army throughout the war.

The former slave boy Matthew Lyon rose to the rank of colonel in Ethan Allen's militia and fought the British at the battles of Bennington and Saratoga.

One of the founders of the state of Vermont, he was elected to its assembly and later to the U.S. Congress, where the eponymous firebrand wrestled a Federalist on the floor of the House of Representatives. He was the first American to be indicted under President John Adams' Sedition Act, for publishing material against central Federal government and Adams. Forced to run for Congress from a jail cell, Lyon was overwhelmingly re-elected and returned to a tumultuous hero's welcome in Vermont.

The colonies of Rhode Island, New Jersey and Maryland declared White slaves eligible to enlist in the Continental Army without their master's consent. Though such decrees had the effect of granting the freedom of those slaves who fought, the American

Revolution did not result in a prohibition of the institution of White slavery itself. In rhetoric it was conceded that White slavery was "contrary to the idea of liberty" but the system remained profitable and many Southern and middle colony White slaves had not been allowed to join the Revolutionary Army and they remained in bondage. The importation of White slaves was resumed after the American Revolution on much the same basis as it had existed before, with the exception of convict slave-labor. In 1788 the Continental Congress urged the states to ban the importation of convict slave labor. (W.C. Ford, *Journals of the Continental Congress, 1774-1789;* entry for Sept. 16, 1788).

White Slave Rebellions

Fear of rebellion by White slaves led to the passage of a Virginia law to suppress "unlawful meetings" and directed that "all masters of ffamilies be enjoyned to take especial care that servants do not depart from their houses on Sundays or any other dayes without particular lycence from them."

Individual acts of rebellion by White slaves were constant and many slavemasters were killed. "...unrest among white servants was more or less chronic." (Bridenbaugh, p. 108). "During the third quarter of the seventeenth century, impoverished white laborers had kept the (Virginia) province on the brink of civil war." (Ekirch, p. 133). In the Caribbean colonies White slaves revolted by burning the sugar cane of the slavemasters "to the utter ruin and undoing of their Masters."

Lured to colonial America with the promise of a teaching job, Thomas Hellier was instead enslaved as a field worker. That betrayal combined with the viciousness of his slavemaster's wife led him to kill the slavemaster's entire family with an axe in 1678. Hellier was believed to have been inspired by Bacon's Rebellion two years before.

In 1676 Nathaniel Bacon led an uprising in Virginia. A small army of former White slaves and fugitive White slaves joined with the 30 year old Indian fighter Bacon against the House of Burgesses and the Governor, sparked by anger at their own penurious condition after having been cheated out of the "head" acreage they were promised and enraged by the Royal government's apathy in the face of murderous Indian raids. There was great fear among the circle of the governor, William Berkeley, that the White slaves of the entire region would rise with Bacon and "carry all beyond remedy to destruction."

Bacon's rebels burned down the city of Jamestown, plundered the plantations and expelled Berkeley. Bacon died suddenly, allegedly of dysentery, on Oct. 26, at the height of the insurrection. "...an incredible number of the meanest (poorest) of people were everywhere armed to assist him and his cause," and these fought on through the winter, until the last of them were captured or killed by January of 1677.

Such combinations of White slaves and landless White freemen were referred to as a "giddy multitude" with the potential for overthrowing the dominance of the planter grandees. "Governor Berkeley despaired of ever subduing a White underclass of 'people where six parts of seven are poor, indebted, discontented and armed." (Ekirch, p. 134).

Other White slave rebellions included the risings of 1634 which took 800 troops to put down, and 1647 in which 18 leaders of the White revolt were tortured and hung.

The rulers of Barbados passed a proclamation in 1649, "An act for an Annual Day of Thanksgiving for our deliverance from the last Insurrection of servants." Richard Ligon was an eyewitness to this White slave plot on Barbados:

"Their sufferings being grown to a great height, and their daily complainings to one another.... being spread throughout the Island; at the last, some amongst them, whose spirits were not able to endure such slavery, resolved to break through it, or die in the act; and so conspired with some others... so that a day was appointed to fall upon their Masters and cut all their throats..." (Ligon, p.45).

And in Virginia: "After mid-century the number of runaway (White) servants increased steadily, and in 1661 and 1663, servants in two separate (Virginia) counties took up arms and demanded freedom. The first episode occurred in York County, where servants complained of 'hard usage'... Isaac Friend, their leader, planned to bring together about forty servants. They would then 'get arms' and march through the country, raising recruits by urging servants 'who would be for liberty, and free from bondage,' to join them. Once a large enough force had been aroused, the rebels would go through the country and kill those that made any opposition, and they would either be free or die for it" (Levine, p. 56).

More White slave "plots" and revolts occurred in 1686 and 1692 including a rebellion by the "Independents," an insurgent group of White Protestant slaves and freedmen who revolted against Maryland's Catholic theocracy.

Revolts on board ships carrying White slaves to America were particularly fiercesome. On at least six occasions White slaves seized ships long enough to neutralize their crews and make good their escape, or they took control completely, "often with bloody consequences for masters and crews." Forty Irish slaves in 1735 ran a vessel aground off Nova Scotia and executed the entire ship's company. Encountering a neqro on shore, they slit his throat "from ear to ear."

In 1751 English slaves from Liverpool shot the ship's captain, drove a spike through the jaw of one of the crew, locked up the remainder and fled the vessel for the North Carolina coast, where they successfully made their escape. (Ekirch, p. 109).

At the age of five James Dalton had watched his father hanged at Tyburn gallows. Around 1720, as a teenager, he was seized, sentenced to enslavement in America and placed aboard the ship Honour, bound for Virginia. During a storm at sea, he and fifteen other White slaves battled the captain and crew for control of the ship. They won and made their way to the Spanish coast and freedom after a two week voyage.

"Certain runaways were fiercely determined. The fugitive Jeffe Walden, when threatened with capture by his master's blacksmith, proclaimed that he 'was upon hasty business' and 'no man should stop' him. 'Choosing rather to suffer death than go back... Similarly, John Oulton, after being overtaken by an overseer in Baltimore County, grabbed a knife and stabbed his pursuer in the chest." White slaves who were caught often continued to seek their freedom. "References in newspaper advertisements to iron collars and fresh whippings attested to their dogged persistence."

One ad for a fugitive White slave stated, "The fellow may be easily known, being cut on his back and arms from a late whipping he had, on his attempting to run away, the night before." (Ekirch, p. 203).

In 1721 White slaves were arrested while attempting to seize an arsenal at Annapolis, Maryland, the arms to be used in an uprising against the Planters. In Florida in 1 768 White slaves revolted at the Turnbull plantation in New Smyrna. The government needed two ships full of troops and cannon to put down the revolt.

A White field slave, Jeremiah Swift, had been hoeing tobacco hills when one of his master's sons demanded that he hoe "a thousand hills before night." Swift attacked him with the hoe, bashing his head in. He then pursued another son, killing him as well. Grabbing an axe and a knife, he entered the master's plantation home, killing one of his daughters and stabbing another. The master, John Hatherly, was not at home at the time. (*Pennsylvania Gazette,* May 9, May 16, June 27, 1751).

Perhaps the most perversely eloquent testimony to the sort of rage and madness that was engendered by treating White men like beasts, was offered by a White slave in Maryland. Worked half to death, he stopped his labor, grabbed an axe and in the familiar pattern, headed for his master's plantation house, where he confronted the man's wife. His intent was not homicide, however. Laying his own hand on his mistress' kitchen cutting block, he brought his axe down full force upon it. "Now make me work if you can!" he screamed, as he threw his severed hand at her. (*Maryland Gazette,* April 17, May 1, 1751).

"If the servant class threw up one radical hero, it was Cornelius Bryan, an Irish servant, imprisoned for mutiny on countless occasions and regularly whipped by the hangman for assembling servants and publicly making anti-planter remarks." (Beckles, "Rebels and Reactionaries," p. 18)

The British colonial government was not adverse to calling on unlikely policemen to suppress White slave revolts: Blacks. Blacks were admitted to the colonial militia responsible for policing White slaves. The aristocratic planters had felt the necessity to "arm part of their blackmen" to assist in suppressing White slave revolts. (Beckles, "Rebels and Reactionaries," p. 17).

Armed Black militias patrolled the Carolinas from the end of the 17th century to at least 1710 when Thomas Nairne reported that Blacks continued to be members of British colonial militias organized by local governments.

In Maryland in 1715, a reward was offered to American Indians who were recruited as bounty hunters to capture runaway Whites and return them to their masters, "For the better discovery of and encouragement of our neighbor Indians to seize, apprehend or take up any runaway servants." It was decreed that for every fugitive White laborer the Indians caught and brought "before a magistrate, they shall, for a reward, have a match-coat paid him or them, or the value thereof…" (*Maxcy's Laws of Maryland,* vol. one, p. 111).

White rebellions foreshadowed the later switch from reliance on masses of White slaves to greater and greater importation of Blacks because of their pliability and passivity. But throughout the 17th and much of the 18th century, the tobacco, sugar and cotton colonies maintained a sizable White slave population. Negro slaves simply cost too much to import and purchase. Whites were cheaper and more expendable— until they began to fight. "…planters, especially in the South, eventually elected to replace the restive white servants with the more identifiable and presumably less criminal black slaves." (Van der Zee, p. 266).

The toughness and sturdiness of the White slaves who not only fought in Bacon's Rebellion but took the worst duty in the French and Indian wars and the American Revolution may have been due in part to the presence of convicts in their ranks. "…convicts provided the colonies with cannon fodder against the Spanish, the French and the Indians." (Ekirch, p. 153).

Not all colonists looked with favor on the reliance upon White convict-slave-labor to build America. Benjamin Franklin opposed White slavery and supposedly referred to White convict-slaves shipped to America as "human serpents."

While British convicts frequently rebelled against their enslavement, their transportation to America did not generally result in a crime wave, because most of them were not professional criminals at all, as the aristocracy had alleged, but "surplus" British farmhands and urban poor people who had been labeled as criminals and swept from Britain to furnish the cheap White labor essential to the American colonial enterprise. "Surviving court records show that in areas (of colonial America) where convicts were imported in large numbers they committed very few offenses... crime never became a major social problem before the Revolution." (Ekirch, pp. 4 and 186).

"Overall most of the convicts were not the 'atrocious villains' so often spoken of..." (Shaw, p.164). When attempts were made to abolish White slavery and thereby stop the flow of both kidnapped and convict labor into colonial America, the measures were generally voted down, as when in 1748 Virginia's Burgesses upheld the Act of 1705— which legitimized White slavery under a veil of legal phraseology. White convict-labor was used for the very harshest and life-threatening jobs others would not do— such as fighting the Indians and French in Arctic conditions with few— if any— firearms.

(Benjamin Franklin had been apprenticed at age 12 to his printer-brother. The term of his indenture was to have been for nine years, but he managed to have his contract voided while his brother was in jail for seditious publishing. As a young man, Franklin was once mistaken for a fugitive White slave, "and in danger of being taken up on that suspicion").

The notion that Whites are particularly "hardhearted" and "racist" because they upheld a fugitive slave law against Blacks is specious when considered in light of the enactments against rebellious and fugitive White slaves. If a tiny clique of wealthy Whites didn't feel sorry for their own people thus enslaved, and hunted them when they escaped or revolted, why would anyone expect them to exempt negroes from the same treatment?

Sometimes the reverse was true. Whites like Harriet Beecher Stowe were solely concerned with the plight of Blacks and avoided or denied the oppression of Whites. Like the wealthy "liberal" White elite of our time who do nothing for the White poor but campaign tirelessly for the rights of colored people, the Quakers of colonial Philadelphia were early advocates of Black rights and abolition of negro servitude even as some Quakers whipped and brutalized the White slaves they continued to own. (7)

Torture and Murder of White Slaves

White slaves were punished with merciless whippings and beatings. The records of Middlesex County, Virginia relate how a slavemaster confessed "that he hath most uncivilly and inhumanly beaten a (White) female with great knotted whipcord— so that the poor servant is a lamentable spectacle to behold."

"Whippings were commonplace... as were iron collars and chains." (Ekirch, p. 150).

A case in the county from 1655 relates how a White slave was "fastened by a lock with a chain to it" by his master and tied to a shop door and "whipped till he was very bloody." The beating and whipping of White slaves resulted in so many being beaten to death that in 1662 the Virginia Assembly passed a law prohibiting the private burial of White slaves because such burial helped to conceal their murders and encouraged further atrocities against other White slaves.

A grievously ill White slave was forced by his master to dig his own grave, since there was little likelihood that the master would obtain any more labor from him. The White slave's owner "made him sick and languishing as he was, dig his own grave, in which he was laid a few days afterwards, the others being too busy to dig it, *having their hands full in attending to the tobacco."* *(Jaspar*

Danckaerts and Peter Sluyter, Journal of a Voyage to New York and a Tour of Several American Colonies, 1679-1680).

In New England, Nicholas Weekes and his wife deliberately cut off the toes of their White slave who subsequently died. Marmaduke Pierce in Massachusetts severely beat a White slave boy with a rod and finally beat him to death. Pierce was not punished for the murder. In 1655 in the Plymouth Colony a master named Mr. Latham, starved his 14 year old White slave boy, beat him and left him to die outdoors in sub-zero temperatures. The dead boy's body showed the markings of repeated beatings and his hands and feet were frozen solid.

Colonial records are full of the deaths by beating, starvation and exposure of White slaves in addition to tragic accounts such as the one of the New Jersey White slave boy who drowned himself rather than continue to face the unmerciful beatings of his master (*American Weekly Mercury,* Sept. 2-9, 1731).

Henry Smith beat to death an elderly White slave and raped two of his female White slaves in Virginia. John Dandy beat to death his White slave boy whose black and blue body was found floating down a creek in Maryland. Pope Alvey beat his White slave girl Alice Sanford to death in 1663. She was reported to have been "beaten to a Jelly." Joseph Fincher beat his White slave Jeffery Haggman to death in 1664.

John Grammer ordered his plantation overseer to beat his White slave 100 times with a cat-o'-ninetails. The White slave died of his wounds. The overseer, rather than expressing regret at the death he inflicted stated, "I could have given him ten times more." There are thousands of cases in the colonial archives of inhuman mistreatment, cruelty, beatings and the entire litany of *Uncle Tom's Cabin* horrors administered to hapless White slaves.

In Australia, White slave Joseph Mansbury had been whipped repeatedly to such an extent that his back appeared, "quite bare of flesh, and his collar bones were exposed looking very much like two ivory, polished horns. It was with difficulty that we could find another place to flog him. Tony [Chandler, the overseer] suggested to me that we had better do it on the soles of his feet next time." (Robert Hughes, *The Fatal Shore,* p. 115). Hughes describes the fate of White slaves as one of "prolonged and hideous torture."

One overseer in Australia whose specialty was whipping White slaves would say while applying his whip on their backs, "Another half pound mate, off the beggar's ribs." The overseer's face and clothes were described as having the appearance of "a mincemeat chopper, being covered in flesh from the victim's body." (Hughes, p. 115).

In colonial America, in one case, the sole punishment for the murder of a White slave (explained as an accident) consisted of the master and his wife being forbidden from owning any White slaves for a period of three years. A White girl enslaved by a woman called Mistress Ward, was whipped so badly that she died from it. On the finding of a jury that such action was "unreasonable and unchristianlike," Mistress Ward was fined 300 pounds of tobacco.

"...it was no easy task to secure the conviction of a master for the murder of his (White) servant... Convictions of masters for the murder or manslaughter of their servants were definitely the exception. In a preponderance of such trials they were acquitted or let off lightly, often in the face of incontrovertible evidence of guilt" (Morris, pp. 485 and 487).

In 1678 Charles Grimlin, a wealthy American colonial planter, was found guilty of murdering a female White slave he owned. He was pardoned and set free. In the same year a White woman "of low origins," killed her husband, a man of some wealth. The same judge who had pardoned Grimlin sentenced the White woman (who was probably a descendant of White slaves) to be "burned alive according to the law."

Nor should it be concluded that because some trials were held for those masters who murdered their White slaves that this reflected a higher justice than that given to Black slaves.

In thousands of cases of homicide against poor Whites there were no trials whatsoever— murdered White slaves were hurriedly buried by their masters so that the resulting decomposition would prohibit any enquiry into the cause of their deaths. Others just "disappeared" or died from "accidents" or committed "suicide." Many of the high number of so-called "suicides" of White slaves took place under suspicious circumstances, but in every single case the slavemaster was found innocent of any crime. (For acquittals of masters in Virginia or instances of failure to prosecute them for the murder of White slaves, see *Virginia General Court Minutes,* VMH, XIX, 388).

At the same time, White slaves, White servants and poor White working men were forbidden to serve on a jury. Only Whites who owned property could do so. Judges were recruited solely from the propertied class. When the few cases regarding the torture and murder of White slaves reached a court it was not difficult to predict the outcome.

A White orphan boy was kidnapped in Virginia and enslaved under the guise of "teaching him a trade." The boy was able to have the Rappahannock County Court take notice of his slavery: "...an orphan complained on July 2, 1685 that he was held in a severe and hard servitude illegally and that he was taken by one Major Hawkins 'under pretense of giving him learning.' The case came before the court on August 2, but the justices decided that he must continue in the service of his present master." (Jernegan, pp. 159-160).

"They possessed one right— to complain to the planter-magistrates concerning excessively violent abuse. But this right, which by custom was also available to black slaves in some societies, had little or no mitigating effect on the overall nature of their treatment on the estates" (Beckles, *White Servitude,* p. 5. For information on Blacks allowed to accuse White slavemasters in court and who were freed from slavery as a result of hearings before White judges, see the Minutes of Council of March 10, 1654 in the *Lucas manuscripts,* reel 1, f. 92, Bridgetown Public Library, Barbados).

In some cases White slaves were whipped by the authorities just for making a complaint to a court about their master. In Westmoreland County, Virginia in 1724 a White slave received twenty lashes for having complained of mistreatment. In 1738 another Westmoreland White slave, George Smith, was whipped twenty-nine times for making a complaint.

Constables and local magistrates in Virginia to whom mistreated White slaves might appeal were often the same men who enslaved and assaulted them.

It should be recalled that the killing and maiming of White slaves was visited upon them by kinsmen of the same race and religion as their slaves, making the callous disregard for their human rights doubly heinous.

Crackers, Redlegs, Rednecks and Hillbillies

The whole apparatus of the institution of human slavery in English-speaking America, which has been searingly memorialized in the voluminous literature on negro slavery, was first put into place in the enslavement of Whites who were kidnapped in their native land, died on board ship, suffered child slavery and separation of parents from children forever; endured fugitive slave-laws, the banning of White slave meetings and severe and extreme corporal punishment, sometimes unto death.

The motivation for the cover-up of the extent of White slavery by Establishment-funded and approved house scholars is obvious. To admit the true history of White slavery and record it faithfully in modern history is to furnish empirical evidence that White skin does not necessarily embody power or status; that the "poor White," "redneck" of today who is asked to subsidize with his taxes and make sacrifices in his living wage and job prospects, so that Blacks may be "compensated for slavery," in reality owes nobody for anything.

A 1679 colonial census of Whites who fled slavery to scratch out an existence as subsistence and tenant farmers shows that they had to flee to the worst land where they existed in extreme poverty, forming yeoman peasant communities in the hills. It is instructive to note that this White yeomanry was mocked and scorned by both the wealthy White planter elite as well as the negroes. Rich, White plantation owners joined with the negroes in insulting White slaves and poor White people, referring to them as "poor-white earth-scratching scum," "crackers," "redshanks" "redlegs" (forerunner of the "redneck" racial insult current nowadays), "Hill Billys" and "Scotland Johnnies."

"The servants were regarded by the planters as 'white trash" (Eric Williams, *Capitalism and Slavery,* p. 17).

White slaves were taunted in the West Indies by Blacks who would chant the ditty, "Yella hair, speckly face and dey feet brick red" at them. (The epithet "redshanks" developed into the name redlegs which has since become a term for all survivors and descendants of White slaves in the Caribbean region).

Various merchants and aristocrats of the 18th and 19th centuries despised the independence of these survivors of White slavery when they encountered them in the British West Indies. The chief hallmark of the redlegs has been their absolute refusal to interbreed with the negroes and their independent subsistence lifestyle of fishing and gardening. Here is a typical 19th century description of them by an aristocrat:

"...that lowest of all beings, the 'redshanks.' The latter were miserable and degraded white men who, priding themselves on their Caucasian origin, looked with contempt upon the African race." (Sheppard, p. 3).

"A loyalist refugee from Georgia wrote in 1783: 'The Southern colonies are overrun with a swarm of men from the western parts of Virginia and North Carolina, distinguished by the name of Crackers. Many of these people are descended from convicts that were transported from Great Britain to Virginia at different times, and inherit so much profligacy from their ancestors, that they are the most abandoned set of men on earth, few of them having the least sense of religion... During the King's Government these Crackers were very troublesome in the settlements... they also occasioned frequent disputes with the Indians..." (Anthony Stokes, *A View of the Constitution of the British Colonies,* quoted in Ekirch, p. 193).

In 1654 Henry Whistler called the White slaves of Barbados "rubbish, rogues and whores" (*Journal of the West India Expedition*). In England they had been referred to by Edmund Burke as a "swinish multitude," by Samuel Johnson as "rabble" and by Sir Josiah Child as "loose, vagrant... vicious... people."

While the public articulation of such negative epithets against Black people as "nigger" is regarded as a sacrilegious incitement to "hate crimes," hateful terms of abuse of White people such as "redneck" and "cracker" are gleefully recited in newspapers and television today and express the contempt which a powerful segment of our society continues to feel toward White working and poor people.

It is a travesty of historiography that out of deference to the vast political house-of-cards that has been built upon the myth that only Blacks were merchandised in the Atlantic slave trade, historians have failed to consistently describe White chattel by the scientifically accurate term for their condition, that of slave. By avoiding this description, many academics have perpetuated the propaganda of the plutocracy which inflicted these horrors upon White humanity.

Powerful colonial land companies motivated by gigantic profits were loath to admit truths subversive of the fictions which permitted the smooth functioning of "business as usual." The label given the White laborer in bondage was crucial to a correct understanding of his condition.

In the founding era of colonial America, both White and Black slaves were referred to as "servants." Once the term slavery came into universal usage (a word derived from the enslavement of Slavic peoples), objective observers of the time who were without mercenary ties to the traffic in White "servants" called them slaves: "Contemporary observers described it as 'white slavery' and referred to indentured servants as 'White slaves." (Beckles, p. 71).

"Some who in England lived fine and brave,
was there like horses forc'd to trudge and slave.
Some view'd our Limbs turned us around,
Examining like Horses we were sound.

"Some felt our hands others our Legs and Feet,
And made us walk to see we were compleat,
Some view'd our Teeth to see if they was good,
And fit to Chaw our hard and homely food.

"No shoes nor stocking had I for to wear
Nor hat, nor cap, my hands and feet went bare.
Thus dressed unto the fields I did go,
Among Tobacco plants all day to hoe.

"Till twelve or one o'clock a grinding corn,
And must be up at day break in the morn.
For I was forc'd to work while I could stand,
Or hold the hoe within my feeble hands.

"Forc'd from Friends and Country to go…
Void of all Relief… Sold for a Slave…"

—From the writing of White slave John Lawson, 1754. (Quoted in Van Der Zee, *Bound Over*).

"Honored Father:
...O Dear Father... I am sure you'll pity your distressed daughter. What we unfortunate English people suffer here is beyond the probability of you in England to conceive.

"Let it suffice that I am one of the unhappy number toiling day and night, and very often in the horse's druggery, with only the comfort of hearing me called, 'You, bitch, you did not do half enough.'

"Then I am tied up and whipped to that degree that you'd not serve an animal. I have scarce any thing but Indian corn and salt to eat and that even begrudged. Nay, many negroes are better used...

"...after slaving after Master's pleasure, what rest we can get is to wrap ourselves up in a blanket and lay upon the ground. This is the deplorable condition your poor Betty endures..."

-From a letter by White slave Elizabeth Sprigs in Maryland to her father John Sprigs in London, England, September 22, 1756. (Public Record Office, London, England, High Court of Admiralty).

KIDNAPPER. Originally one who stole or decoyed children or apprentices from their parents or masters, to send them to the colonies; called also spiriting: but now used for all recruiting crimps for the king's troops, or those of the East India company, and agents for indenting servants for the plantations., &c.

Capt. Francis Grose, *Dictionary of the Vulgar Tongue* [1796]

kidnapper. A stealer of human beings, esp. of children; orig. for exportation to the plantations of North America: 1666, Anon., *Leathermore's Advice* (known also as *The Nicker Nicked*), in form *kidnapper;* 1676, Coles; 1698, B.E.; 1707, J. Shirley; 1723, D. Defoe, *Colonel Jacque.* The term > s. Ca. 1750; S.E., ca. 1830. It is to be noted that kidnappers worked in gangs: witness D. Defoe, *Colonel Jacque,* 'He was got among a Gang of Kidnappers, as they were then call'd, being a Sort of wicked Fellows that us'd to Spirit Peoples Children away, that is to snatch them up in the Dark, and stopping their Mouths, carry them to such Houses where they had Rogues, ready to receive them, and so carry them on Board Ships bound to *Virginia,* and sell them'. Lit., a child-stealer, a stealer of children: see **kid,** n., 1, and **napper.**

Eric Partridge, *A Dictionary of the Underworld*

A GANG OF MEN AND WOMEN TRANSPORTS BEING MARCHED FROM NEWGATE TO BLACKFRIARS

Chained neck to neck and hand to hand these wretches were led through the streets to Blackfriars Stairs, where they were taken aboard a barge and carried down the river to the vessel which was to transport them to America

White Slaves

Michael A. Hoffman II *They Were White and They Were Slaves*

Survivors of White Slavery

The Death of Two "Human Brooms"

Poor White children were a very expendable commodity in Georgian and Victorian England, as this period print of an actual chimney-sweeping accident illustrates. Enslaved to a master of chimney sweeps from as young as the age of four, White boys were forced to climb inside suffocating and cramped flues and clean them. They received no pay, begged their food and slept in cellars. Many died from accidents, beatings and cancer brought on from constant contact with ash and cinder which they had no opportunity to wash from their skin.

In the illustration above, two "climbing boys" have been crushed and suffocated after the collapse of the chimney's masonry. The man on the right with the pick is a "builder," who has been summoned to extricate the children. One lies dead on the floor (bottom, left), mourned perhaps by a servant of the house, since these White slaves were almost all orphans or the kidnapped children of paupers. The other boy remains stuck in the flue. His master is attempting to pull him from the rubble by his foot and leg, as the lady of the house looks on.

Thousands of White children slaved as sweeps. The British House of Lords repeatedly refused to outlaw the use of White children under the age of ten, or reform the trade in any way. The Lords contended that to do so would interfere with "property rights."

A Childhood in the Factory

The British and American Factory System of the Industrial Revolution was staffed mainly by enslaved ('indentured') White children who were forced to work, as children had never worked before"— sixteen hours a day, locked into a building, without breaks (except to go to the "necessary"). Food was taken standing up, while tending the primitive machinery which mutilated tens of thousands of children. For falling asleep or talking, White girls and boys were beaten with a leather strap or a "billyroller," a murderous iron bar.

The photograph above is of American girls who worked a seventy hour week at a factory in South Carolina in the early 1900's.

Alabama Sharecropper — 1936

The hardscrabble life of rural White Americans, many of them descendants of White slaves, has been made a subject of comedy, scorn, dismissal and denial. They are called "rednecks, crackers" and White "trash." Their history has been suppressed, their heritage and way of life condemned.

The sharecropper pictured above was not allowed to grow so much as a patch of vegetable garden for his family's needs, on the land he worked for the Margraves brothers, lest it take away even a few hundred square feet from the cotton he cultivated and picked on their behalf.

End Notes

1. The Oxford English dictionary traces the word slave (also *sclaue, sclave, sclayff*) to the medieval Latin *sclavus* which was the name for the Slavs. The German philologists Grimm trace this word for the Slavic peoples and chattel enslavement to late Greek, medieval Latin and German sources in their *Deutsches Worterbuch* under the heading "Sklave."

In early Britain another White nationality bore the same eponymous stigma. The West Saxon word for slave was *Wielisc* (from the Old English *Wealh*), which was also the name for the Celtic or Welsh race but by the ninth century had the distinct meaning in Britain of "slave."

Other words for White slaves which demonstrate the ubiquity of White enslavement include: *esne* and *peow* (Old English). Thrall is an anglicized word taken from Scandinavian sources (in Middle English *thrawl* and in Old English *prael* from the Old Norse *praell*). *Drigil* (Old High German probably derived from the Proto Old Norse *prahilar* and the Proto-Germanic *preghila,* from the Gothic *pragjan*). *Amboot* (Old Swedish); *ambactus* (Celt); *annopoghaer* (Old Danish); *anauoigr* (Old Icelandic); *mansalsmaor* (Old Norse; literally "man-saleman").

lasyr (esyr) and *rab* are the Russian words for slave. The English word robot is derived from the Russian word for work, *rabota,* "the labor of a slave" (Hellie, p. 711) which says much about the legacy of White slavery in Russia. The Muslims called White slaves by the Arabic version of the word Slav, *saqaliba*.

2. One remarkable former member of the "poor White trash" of the South who exhibited a lifelong solidarity with his own kind, was the phenomenally successful Andrew Johnson, military governor of Tennessee, U.S. Senator, Vice-President and 17th President of the United States.

A prevailing myth has it that Lincoln was assassinated because hidden powers knew he would be lenient to the South during Reconstruction. This view is exploded when one studies the background and views of his successor to the presidency, who was everything to the defeated Southern people (though not to their Planter-dominated Confederate leadership, who he generally despised), that the myth-makers claim Lincoln would have been.

President Johnson was impeached mainly through the partisan efforts of politicians such as Rep. Thaddeus Stevens and Sen. Charles Sumner, precisely because Johnson refused to cooperate in the collective "Reconstruction" punishment of poor White people in the South.

Andrew Johnson was born in Raleigh, North Carolina, where at the age of ten he was apprenticed to the Selby tailor shop and ordered to work twelve hours a day, until he was 21 years of age.

"Andrew could hardly miss feeling the striking contrast between himself and the (White) elite... the aristocrats' contempt was scarcely hidden. When Andrew and his cousins once ran across the path between the house of John Devereaux and that of his son, Devereaux sent his coachman to whip the boys back to their shanty... the whip was habitually used on those the Devereaux called 'poor white trash.' (Hans L. Trefousse, *Andrew Johnson, A Biography,* p. 21)

After enduring nearly six years of apprenticeship, Johnson fled Raleigh. A ten dollar reward was posted for his capture. By law, no other employer in North Carolina was allowed to give him work. As long as he remained in North Carolina he was subject to arrest and in danger of capture. Johnson fled to Tennessee where he went into business for himself and eventually became a leader of men.

Johnson has been described as having "...strongly held predilections for the (White) laboring classes and... deepest prejudice against the blacks." (Trefousse, p. 223) As military governor of Tennessee during the war Johnson protected the white poor (Trefousse, pp. 164-165).

Johnson was a staunch Unionist, strictly devoted to preserving the country as one nation. Lincoln selected him as his vice-president in 1864 because Johnson was a border-state Southerner, a constituency which was Lincoln's crucial power base and one he sought to fortify with Johnson, never expecting the latter would ever be anything more than a figurehead.

That Lincoln and Johnson held very different views on racial matters was evident when Lincoln introduced Johnson to a Black leader at the inauguration: "Frederic Douglass recalled that when Lincoln pointed him out to Johnson prior to the ceremonies, the vice president responded at first with a bitter expression of contempt... Douglass concluded right then and there that the Tennessean was no friend of the black race." (Trefousse, p. 190). Perhaps Johnson had read Douglass' book, *Life and Times* which denounced the poor White people of Maryland as being "of the lowest order" (Douglass, p. 27).

As president, Johnson ordered the removal of negro troops from East Tennessee and Mississippi. He also "...reanimated (White) Southern resistance and fatally undermined efforts to integrate the (negro) freedmen into society...

"According to the *Cincinnati Enquirer,* Johnson wrote to Governor Thomas C. Fletcher of Missouri, 'This is a country for white men and by God, as long as I am President, it shall be a government for white men."

In 1859, while U.S. Senator, Johnson "...asserted that the famous phrase in the Declaration of Independence proclaiming that all men were created equal could not apply to negroes "...the 17th president unquestionably undermined the Reconstruction process... What defeated him during his term in the White House was not so much his lack of formal education, nor even his tactlessness, but his failure to outgrow his Jefferson-Jacksonian background. Johnson's continued indentification with an America of small farmers and 'mechanics,' his attachment to a strict construction of the Constitution that was no longer in vogue, his refusal to adjust his racial views to the needs of the Republican party, and his persistent belief in the agrarian myth, blinded him to the realities of the postCivil War U.S...

"Considering the effect of his policies upon the South, he had achieved at least in the long run what he wanted, the continued existence of viable Southern state governments within the Union and the maintenance of White supremacy." (Trefousse, pp. 225, 233, 236, 119, 378-379, 352).

President Johnson vetoed the "Civil Rights" Bill of 1866. "To protest... the Convention of Colored Men met in Washington... and chose a delegation to take their grievances directly to the president. Both (Frederic) Douglass and his son Lewis were members of the delegation. Douglass, as chief spokesman... said that... black people... should be given the vote 'with which to save ourselves.'

"...Johnson, once an indentured servant learning the craft of tailoring ...with 'repressed anger,'... declared, 'moving very near to

Mr. Douglass'... (that) poor whites and... blacks had always been bitter enemies and if they were 'thrown together at the ballot box' a race war would ensue... Johnson (told them)... black people should emigrate. (He would have been delighted to load the first ship with the delegation he was addressing)." -William S. McFeely, *Frederic Douglass,* pp. 247-248.

Radical Republican Massachusetts Senator Charles Sumner also personally interceded with President Johnson to demand the vote for negroes. After meeting with Johnson, "Sumner wrote, 'Much that he said was painful from its prejudice ...and perversity."

President Johnson was so contemptuous of the negrophile Senator that in the course of their discussion he "...used the Senator's hat as a spittoon...

"He was determined to frustrate Congressional Reconstruction and to protect Southern whites from what he considered the horrors of full racial equality." -"The Man Who Succeeded Lincoln," *New York Times,* July 29, 1989.

3. Negro involvement in the enslavement of their fellow Blacks was extensive: "...in Africa... down to the 1930s, the various tribes continued to raid one another to capture slaves both for domestic use and to sell to outsiders. Moreover, in spite of the picture presented in Alex Haley's Roots, white slave traders almost never entered the interior in pursuit of prey but rather purchased their cargo from Africans at the ocean front; coastal Africans would not allow Europeans either into or through their own countries... Before the appearance of the (Suzanne) Miers and (Igor) Kopytoff and Meillassoux volumes (*Slavery in Africa: Anthropological and Historical Perspectives*), some scholars claimed that slavery in Africa was a response to the international slave trade, but it is now obvious that (Black) slavery was an old domestic institution that was adapted for supplying the international market when it developed." (Hellie, pp. 22 and 24).

4. Prof. Handlin informs us that legislators in Virginia sought to coverup the record of White bondage and its equivalence to negro servitude: "The compiler of the Virginia laws (codifying Black slavery for the first time) then takes the liberty of altering texts to bring earlier legislation into line with his own new notions" (Handlin, p. 216. For examples of alterations to insert the word slave as a reference to Blacks in Virginia when it had not been used to describe them that way before, see Hening, vol. 2, pp. iii, 170, 283, 490).

What was it later lawmakers sought to coverup? The fact that the White ruling class of colonial America had cast their own White people into the same condition as the Blacks, or even worse.

Richard Ligon's eyewitness report of a White slave revolt in Barbados in 1 649 has been regularly referred to down through the years by at least a dozen later historians including Poyer, Oldmixon and Schomburgk, as a rebellion of negro slaves. In their cases this does not seem to have been a matter of deliberate falsification, but rather a complete inability to conceive of Whites as slaves. Ligon had written that the rebels in question had not been able to "endure such slavery" any longer and the later historians automatically assumed that this had to have been a reference to negroes. It is this persistent cognition by categorical preconception that renders much of what passes for colonial historiography in our era inaccurate and misleading.

5. Old English law did have something of a White slave code, based on the concept of "villeinage" from which we derive the words *villain* and *villainy* with their now pejorative connotations.

With the emergence of the English Common Law (1175-1225) came the rise of the writ of novel disseisin which dealt with who was qualified to contest land evictions. The aristocrats who drafted the writ established a category of juridical unfreedom known as villein tenure which could defeat any English peasant's claim to land, no matter how long his family had held it.

At first villain denoted a White peasant (from the French Carolingian word *vilani,* a general description for a peasant dependent upon a lord), and the sense of evil that was attached to the word was largely a construct of the rich who would naturally want their world order to be seen as good and therefore any White kinsman enslaved was seen as "justly deserving" of such treatment and hence had to have been bad, evil, a "villain."

It was as important for the English nobility to make this claim about English slave "villeins" as it was for American colonial merchants to label the Whites they enslaved as criminals and traitors or in the common parlance found in original documents of the period, as "rubbish and dung."

The Oxford Dictionary gives the following definition of villainy, "The condition or state of a villein, bondage, servitude, hence base or ignoble condition" (*Compact Edition of the Oxford English Dictionary,* p. 3,631). In other words, the connection between villainy and evil first came about from a premeditated association between the condition of being a slave and the state of being an evil person. Who is it that would benefit from stigmatizing White slaves as evil beings? Who but the slaveholding aristocracy who could then justify any crime they committed against these "villains."

Much of the common understanding of the land swindles perpetrated against the English villein class is derived from the legal treatise, *De Legibus et Consuetudinibus Angliae,* commonly known as *Bracton* after Sir Henry de Bracton.

The *Bracton* code equates the English villein with the Roman *servus* or slave. The *Bracton* code denies all rights to the villein by placing him in the same category as the Roman *servus.*

Villeinage was considered a hereditary condition: "Neither of Duke, earl or lord by ancestry but of villain (vylayne) people" (Bradshaw, *St. Werburge,* 1513). "Thou art of vylayn blood on thy father's side" (Caxton, 1483).

This propaganda-labeling of enslaved Whites may be better understood if we examine the original meaning and the subsequent connotations associated with the use of another name, that of "churl." We call someone a churl today who is badly bred or ill mannered. Yet according to the *Random House Dictionary of the English Language,* originally, a churl was an English "freeman of the lowest rank"— the poorest White who was not a slave.

It is no coincidence that the names for White slaves and White poor came to be linked with evil and bad breeding as part of a self-serving process of appellation manufactured by their rulers.

A revealing display of the opprobrium associated with both words is exhibited in a description by Sir Walter Scott: "Sweeping from the earth some few hundreds of villain churles, who are born but to plow it."

The association of these names with what Scott views as a degraded existence of plowing the earth is a holdover from plutocratic ancient Roman philosophy. "Romans considered manual occupations... as degrading in themselves..." (William Phillips, p. 28), since these were associated in the aristocratic mind with the work of slaves.

Up until recently, European history was largely written from the point of view of institutional Churchianity, the wealthy, the aristocracy and the merchant class, at the expense of the laboring people.

Rodney Hilton further cautions that "historians risk falling into the trap dug for the peasants by the lawyers, for most of our evidence about freedom and serfdom depends on evidence which is a byproduct of the legal... process" (Hilton, "Freedom and Villeinage in England," *Past and Present,* July, 1965).

The creation of an exculpatory nomenclature rigged to justify the depredations of the ruling class against the White poor by establishing an intrinsic relationship between being poor and being evil, is a masterstroke of propaganda. It leads to the internalization of these negative images in the minds of the White poor themselves.

Some memory of these connections and connotations were no doubt extant in the minds of colonial Americans and has surely contributed to the dearth of material on those who survived or were descended from White slavery. "Indentured servitude... gave ordinary whites of the (American) revolutionary generation galling experience of a variety of social oppressions..." (Roediger, p. 30).

The widespread hatred of the appellation "servant" and the refusal to be so called by most Americans, however lowly their station, has been noted by many observers and usually ascribed to the heady Republican sentiments of the newly independent nation. As late as 1839, the English writer Frances Trollope remarked, "It is more than petty treason to the republic to call a free citizen a *servant.*" (*Domestic Manners of the Americans*).

It has been noted that servant was the word for slave in early colonial America. The lawyer John Bristed observed that this perceived linkage between the status of slave and servant was widespread even among Whites in 19th century America: "Bristed commented on the tendency of U.S. citizens toward 'confounding the term *servant* with that of *slave*. There was good reason for such confounding, dating from the early imprecision of colonial usages of *slave* and *servant* right through Noah Webster's inconsistent distinctions between the two terms in his dictionary of 1828..." (Roediger, p. 47)

Given the extent of White slavery in America, which had been largely disguised under the subterfuge of the phrase servant, it is not unreasonable to attribute White working class sensitivity associated with the use of this word, to anger stemming from their memory of enslavement.

In Britain and Europe under the laws of villeinage, survivors and descendants of White slavery were susceptible to discrimination before the law and even re-enslavement:

"The former (White) slaves, now serfs, might gradually shift into another legal category over several generations, or the taint of servility might lose much of its practical meaning as they became de facto independent, but... the descendants of (White) slaves were for centuries considered unfree in a way that other people in equally dependent economic positions were not" (Karras, p. 36).

This stigma was based not only in law but in racial terms: "...the culture of the (medieval) slaveholders created an image of (White) slaves that set them apart, their whole moral character tainted by the fact of enslavement if not by slave ancestry." (Karras, pp. 15-16).

This taint, which the ruling class cleverly asserted was the result of some hereditary defect among White slaves, has been applied to many nations of White peoples from the Slavs to the Irish, Welsh and Scottish. The defect attached to White "slave blood" by their rulers served as an effective device for: 1. Keeping descendants of White slaves from seeking redress for past wrongs.

2. Being ashamed to identify their heritage and background in the form of written memorialization. 3. Serving as a neat propaganda justification for the continuing privileges and governance of the aristocracy.

This pattern is occasionally overturned when we examine unfiltered folk literature or music. For example, in such 13th century Icelandic folk sagas as the *Frostbroeora* and the *Laxdoela,* White slaves are portrayed as fair and Nordic in general appearance and possessed of great personal courage and honor.

6. Abraham Lincoln's use of the Bible, which according to his law partner he did not believe, to justify rights for negro slaves, is another example of this masterful politician's distortion of fact. While it is true that Galatians 3:28 contains the famous passage about there being "neither slave nor free... in Christ Jesus," this statement is meant to have only a spiritual application. The passage also contains the statement that there is neither male nor female in Christ, but I rather doubt St. Paul intended to sanction transvestitism or homosexuality. In Ephesians 6:5 slaves are ordered to obey their masters "with fear and trembling as unto Christ."

In considering the Biblical stand on slavery, it is necessary to differentiate Biblical laws concerning the enslavement of aliens and Israelites. The former could be permanent, the latter was to be temporary, even though many who claimed to be the Christian heirs of the Israelites acted otherwise.

In America, those who enslaved Blacks and disparaged the manual laborer, generally did not derive their philosophy from Biblical sources, however; that legacy falls in the camp of ancient Rome (see J. Drew Harrington, "Classical Antiquity and the Proslavery Argument," *Slavery and Abolition,* May, 1989).

Southern planters did justify the bondage of the negro with Biblical arguments, but this was usually a rejoinder to abolitionist attacks, rather than the main source of enslavement praxis. It is chiefly from the aristocratic notions of the Romans toward manual labor that the classic mindset of the modern slaver in the West evolved. These concepts differ considerably from the status of the manual laborer in the Bible. Jesus Christ, the "King of Kings," toiled as a carpenter for most of his life.

7. Harriet Beecher Stowe was one of the great hypocrites of the 19th century, a pious fraud whose legacy of malignant hatred for her own kind has infected many another White man and woman to this day.

During her triumphal 1853 tour of Britain in the wake of the publication of *Uncle Tom's Cabin,* Stowe was the guest of the Duchess of Sutherland, a woman of vast wealth who had an interest in the "betterment of the negro."

The Sutherland wealth was based in part on one of the most criminal land-grabs in British history. The Sutherlands had seized the ancient holdings of the traditional clans of Scotland and burned the Highland "crofters" (farmers) off their lands, resulting in pauperism and in many cases, outright starvation of Scottish women and children (Henry C. Carey, *The Slave Trade, Domestic and Foreign,* pp. 204-209; John Prebble, *The Highland Clearances,* pp. 288-295). At one point the Sutherlands even hired armed guards to prevent famine-stricken Scottish Highlander "rabble" from catching fish in the Sutherland's well-stocked salmon and trout rivers (Prebble, p. 293).

When Harriet Beecher Stowe returned to America she wrote a glowing account of the Sutherlands in her travel book *Sunny Memories,* specifically praising them for their "enlightened land policies" in Scotland, which she described as, "an almost sublime instance of the benevolent employment of superior wealth and power in shortening the struggles of advancing civilization" (Cunliffe, p. 18, Prebble, p. 292). In response to Stowe's appalling whitewash of the crimes committed against the Scottish Highlanders, a London newspaper described *Uncle Tom's Cabin* as a "downright imposture" and "ranting, canting nonsense." (Cunliffe, Ibid.).

Glossary of Terms

Apprentice. A journeyman or master craftsman, whose education is primarily derived "on the job," under the guidance of the master, rather than in a classroom or from a book. Payment for being taught is often in the form of the labor the apprentice performs for the master.

Barbadosed. 17th century. A term for White dissidents shipped into slavery in America for political resistance to the English government. Originally coined in connection with Cavaliers who resisted the Puritan Protectorate of Oliver Cromwell and were transported into slavery in the British colony of Barbados on his orders.

Churl. The lowest rank of Freeman in medieval England.

Duty Boys. 17th century. A macabre term for the most wretched White child slaves, orphans as well as those who were taken from parents under color of law, who were shipped into slavery in America.

Called "Duty Boys" after the children imprisoned in London awaiting shipment to Virginia for enslavement, some of them as young as eight years old, who in January of 1620 rose up during their confinement at Bridewell in horror of their kidnapping. Their rebellion was put down, possibly accompanied by the murder of one of them. In February of 1620 they were chained aboard the ship *Duty* and conveyed to America. By 1625 all but five were dead.

Children labeled Duty Boys were considered the living dead, since their enslavement in Virginia or the West Indies was regarded as a veritable death sentence by the English people and certainly by their parents, who never saw them alive again.

Enticers. Whites who urged White slaves to flee or who assisted fugitive White slaves. Enticers could be flogged with thirty lashes.

Indenture. 1. (Also Indentures, Indentured, Indented). Articles of a legally-binding nature selling a person for a fixed period of time, usually in return for being taught a trade or skill. Traditionally, an indentured laborer has little recourse to complaints regarding length of hours, nature of work or condition of accommodation.

2. A euphemism for the life-long enslavement of Whites in British America.

Kidnapped. Originally, "Kid *nabbed.*" The stealing of White children into slavery in America, practiced on a mass scale as a virtual industry in the British isles in the 17th and 18th centuries.

Redemptioners. Also known as "Free-willers." Those who voluntarily indentured themselves, often in return for boat passage to America.

Redshanks. A derisive term used by both Blacks and White planters to describe White slaves of British origin whose limbs reddened in the sun of the southern colonies. A nearly universal term of abuse. Forerunner of the contemporary insult, "redneck."

Slave. Originally, Slav. A White person of East European (Slavic) descent. (See endnote number one).

Spirits. Kidnappers. For a fee, spirits would assault or "trepan" (trap) White men, women and children aboard slaveships bound for the colonies. The kidnapped Whites would seem to disappear, so quickly were they taken, hence they were said to have been "spirited." These victims were given "Kidnapper's indentures" (forged contracts) or no indentures whatever. In either case they were enslaved usually for life upon arrival, "according to the custom of the country" (i.e. local ordinances created, in many cases, by White slave merchants).

Transported. Also "transportation." A British person carried away to a distant country involuntarily, usually by order of the government. To be "sentenced to transportation" to the colonies was tantamount to being sentenced to slavery. Establishment historians have claimed that this was a mercy since the "felons" would otherwise have been hanged at Tyburn gallows. This simplistic view overlooks two facts:

1. The definitions of "felon" and "convict" in this period were entirely constructed by the ruling class. For example, in 1 699 the Shoplifting Act extended capital offenses to include any theft from a shop to the value of five shillings. Hence a "convict" was very often a starving boy who had committed the "felony" of stealing food for his brothers and sisters. It does not seem like much of a mercy to take him from his parents and siblings forever to slavery in a foreign land.

2. Even hardened professional criminals feared transportation more than hanging because, unlike some 20th century historians, they were not blind to first-hand accounts from sailors and others that penal enslavement in the colonies was often more horrible than death itself, was in fact a kind of living death:

"I... told him... if he was Transported, there might be a Hundred ways for him that was a Gentleman, and a bold enterprising Man to find his way back again, and perhaps some Ways and Means to come back before he went.

"He smiled at that Part, and said he should like the last the best of the two, for he had a kind of Horror upon his Mind at being sent over to the Plantations as Romans sent condemn'd Slaves to Work in the Mines; that he thought the Passage into another State, let it be what it would, much more tolerable at the Gallows, and that this was the general Notion of all the Gentlemen who were driven by the Exigence of their Fortunes to take the Road." (Daniel DeFoe, *Moll Flanders,* Penguin classics edition, p. 380).

'...the robber Robert Webber pleaded to be hanged rather than given a transportation... he 'had rather die than live under bondage...' The thief Mary Stanford... pleaded to be hanged rather than transported...

'Such was the wish of a London malefactor after hearing that he would be transported to the West Indies 'to work there at the sugar works... He pleaded that 'he had rather bear strangling for a minute..." (Ekirch, pp. 63-4').

The notion that transportation was a merciful alternative to imprisonment or death in Britain is an erroneous one. In fact, just the opposite obtained. A merciful judge was regarded as one who *did not* transport British people into slavery in America: "...non-capital criminals still enjoyed a good chance of escaping transportation, especially those who impressed courts as objects of mercy.

"...Once guilt was established, judges, too, could show mercy by sentencing offenders to punishments other than transportation...

"...transportation represented... a curse that large numbers of men and women feverishly sought to avoid... (they) commonly requested that other punishments be substituted in transportation's place... A few, when opportunities arose, allowed their bodies to be used for medical research. In 1721, six prisoners volunteered to undergo a smallpox experiment... Similarly, ten years later, Charles Ray, a prisoner in Newgate, offered to let doctors remove his ear drum rather than be transported... Another Englishman, rather than be transported, permitted one of his limbs to be amputated 'to test the styptic medicines discovered by Mr. Thomas Price..." (Ekirch, pp. 30, 62-63; Shaw, p. 34).

For Eleanor Connor, the sentence of convict labor for life in the colonies, where she would never see her children again, was 'next to death itself.' ("Petition of Eleanor Connor to the Archbishop of Canterbury," circa 1748). "No matter how bleak their economic horizons, local connections and familiar surroundings were very important. References in petitions to 'nativity' and 'home' bespoke a deep reluctance to abandon much of what gave meaning to their lives... However harsh the existence of Britain's poor, many at least drew some strength from community ties." (Ekirch, pp. 65 and 161).

In the words of a ballad written by White slaves in Virginia:
"Oh England, sweet England,
I fear I'll ner'er see you more,
And if I do its ten thousand to twenty.
For my fingers they are rotting, and my bones they are sore.
I wander about right down to death's door."
— *Virginny*

Trepan'd. Trapped. Often used in connection with the means used to convey Whites aboard slave ships against their will.

Villain. (Also villein). Medieval. Originally, an enslaved Englishman. From the French-Carolingian *vilani*. (See endnote no. 5).

Yeoman. (Also yeomanry; yeomen). The founders of England. From "yew-man," a member of the citizen-archers, after the premier wood for making bows, the English yew tree. It was the "yew-men" of the Angles and Saxons who used their bows to defeat King Vortigern and the Celtic army and create the country of "Angle-land" (England).

Bibliography

Acts of the Privy Council, Colonial 1613-1783.
Adshead, Joseph, *Distress in Manchester.*
American Weekly Mercury.
Angle, Paul M., *Created Equal: The Complete Lincoln-Douglas Debates of 1858.*
Annesley, James, *Memoirs of an Unfortunate Young Nobleman Returned from Thirteen Years Slavery in America.*
Ashley, M., *Financial and Commercial Policy Under Cromwell's Protectorate.* Ayearst, Morley, *The British West Indies.*
Ayers, Edward L., *Vengeance and Justice: Crime and Punishment in the Nineteenth Century American South.*
Baines, Edward, *History of the Cotton Manufacture.*
Ballagh, J.C., *White Servitude in the Colony of Virginia.*
Bassett, John S., *Slavery and Servitude in the Colony of North Carolina.*
Beckles, Hilary McD., *Natural Rebels.*
Beckles, Hilary McD., "Plantation Production and White Proto-Slavery," *The Americas, vol. 41, 1985.*
Beckles, Hilary McD., "Rebels and Reactionaries: The Political Responses of White Laborers to Planter-Class Hegemony in 17th Century Barbados," *Journal of Caribbean History, vol. 15, 1981.*
Beckles, Hilary McD., *White Servitude and Black Slavery in Barbados, 1627-1715.*
Bellamy, Joyce and Savilee, John, *Dictionary of Labour Biography.*
Berlin, Ira, *Slaves Without Masters: The Free Negro in the Antebellum South.* Biddle, Henry D., (editor), *Extracts from the Journal of Elizabeth Drinker.*

Breen, T.H., "A Changing Labor Force and Race Relations in Virginia, 1660-1710," *Journal of Social History, no. 7, (1973).*

Bridenbaugh, Carl and Roberta, *No Peace Beyond the Line: The English in the Caribbean, 1624-1690.*

Bromberg, Eric I., "Wales and the Medieval Slave Trade," *Speculum* no. 17, 1942.

Brown, Alexander, *The First Republic in America.*

Brownson, Orestes, "The Laboring Classes," *in Religion, Reform and Revolution.*

Burn, James D., *Three Years Among the Working Classes in he U.S. During the War.*

Burton, Thomas, *Parliamentary Diary: 1656-59.*

Calder, Isabel M., *Colonial Captives, Marches and Journeys.*

Calendar of State Papers, Colonial Series, America and West indies, 1574-1733.

Calendar of State Papers, Domestic, 1547-1704.

Campbell, John, *Negro-Mania.*

Carey, Henry C., *The Slave Trade, Domestic and Foreign.*

Carlyle, Thomas, "Occasional Discourse on the Negro Question," in *Fraser's Magazine* (Dec., 1849). Reprinted 1971 as *The Nigger Question* (Appleton-Century-Crofts).

Channing, Edward, *History of the United States.*

Chase, L. B., *English Serfdom and American Slavery.*

Child, Josiah, *A New Discourse of Trade.*

Chitwood, Oliver, *A History of Colonial America.*

Chvet, Stanley F., *Lopez of Newport.*

Cobden, John C., *The White Slaves of England.*

Connecticut Board of Commissioners of Common Schools, *Legal Provision Respecting the Education and Employment of Children in Factories.*

Cruickshank, Marjorie, *Children and Industry.*

Crumpe, Samuel, *An Essay on the Best Means of Providing Employment For the People.*

Cunliffe, Marcus, *Chattel Slavery and Wage Slavery.*

Dalby, Thomas, *An Historical Account of the Rise and Growth of the West Indies Colonies.*

Danckaerts, Jaspar and Sluyter, Peter, *Journal of a Voyage to New York and a Tour of Several American Colonies, 1679-1680.*

Darvall, F.O., *Popular Disturbances and Public Order in Regency England.*

Davies, Wendy, *Wales in the Early Middle Ages.*

Davis manuscript, *Royal Commonwealth Society Archives.*

Davis, David Brion, *The Problem of Slavery in the Age of Revolution.*

Davis, David Brion, *Slavery and Human Progress.*

Defoe, Daniel, *Colonel Jack.*

Defoe, Daniel, *Moll Flanders.*

Dodd, William, *The Factory System Illustrated.*

Donnan, Elizabeth, *Documents Illustrative of the History of the Slave Trade to America. Douglass, Frederic, Life and Times.*

Driver, Cecil, *Tory Radical: The Life of Richard Oastler.*

Dulles, Foster Rhea, *Labor in America, A History.*

Dunlop, Jocelyn and Denham, Richard, *English Apprenticeship and Child Labour.*

Dunn, Richard S., *Sugar and Slaves: The Rise of the Planter Class in the English West Indies, 1624-1713.*

Eadon, John, (editor), *Memoirs of Pere Labat, 1693-1705.* Eddis, William, *Letters from America.*

Egerton manuscript, *British Museum.*

Ekirch, A. Roger, *Bound for America: The Transportation of British Convicts into the Colonies, 1718-1775.*

Emmer, P.C., *Colonialism and Migration: Indentured Labor Before and After Slavery.*

Esson, D.M.R., *The Curse of Cromwell: A History of the Ironside Conquest of Ireland, 1649-1653.*

Evans, Lloyd, and Nicholls, P., *Convicts and Colonial Society.*

Everett, Susanne, *History of Slavery.*

Fielden, John, *The Curse of the Factory System.*
Finch, John, *Rise and Progress of the General Trades Union of New York.* Fitzhugh, George, *Sociology for the South.*
Fladeland, Betty, *Abolitionists and Working-Class Problems in the Age of Industrialization.* Fleet, Beverly (ed.), *Virginia Colonial Abstracts.*
Fogel, Robert and Engerman, Stanley L., *Time on the Cross.*
Foner, Eric, *Reconstruction: America's Unfinished Revolution, 1863-1877.*
Ford, W.C., ed., *Journals of the Continental Congress, 1774-1789.*
Foster, Charles I., *An Errand of Mercy.*
Fraser, Walter J. Jr., "Reflections of 'Democracy' in Revolutionary South Carolina? The Composition of Military Organizations and the Attitudes and Relationships of the Officers and Men, 1775-1780," in *The Southern Common People.*
Galenson, David W., *Traders, Planters and Slaves.*
Galenson, David W., *White Servitude in Colonial America.*
Geiser, K.F., *Redemptioners and Indentured Servants in the Colony and Commonwealth of Pennsylvania.*
Genovese, Eugene D., "Rather Be a Nigger Than a Poor White Man': Slave Perceptions of Southern Yeomen and Poor Whites," in *Toward a New View of America.* Genovese, Eugene D., *Roll, Jordan Roll: The World the Slaves Made.* Genovese, Eugene D., *The World the Slaveholders Made.*
Glickstein, Jonathan A., *Concepts of Free Labor in Antebellum America.*
Going, Charles B., *David Wilmot: Free-Soiler.*
Gray, Lewis Cecil, *History of Agriculture in the Southern United States to 1860.*
Gray, Ralph and Wood, Betty, "The Transition from Indentured to Involuntary Servitude in Colonial Georgia," *Explorations in Economic History,* October, 1976. Grayson, William J., *The Hireling and the Slave.*
Greenberg, Douglas, *Crime and Law Enforcement in the Colony of New York.*
Hall, Richard, *Acts Passed in the Island of Barbados.*

Halliburton, R., *Red Over Black: Black Slavery Among the Cherokee Indians*.

Hammond, John, *Leah and Rachel, or the Two Fruitful Sisters, Virginia and Maryland*.

Handlin, Oscar and Mary F., "Origins of the Southern Labor System," *William and Mary Quarterly*, April, 1950.

Hanway, Jonas, *A Sentimental History of Chimney-Sweepers*.

Harding, N. Dermott and Bowman, William Dodgson, *Bristol and America: A Record of the First Settlers in the Colonies of North America, 1654-1685*.

Harrington, J. Drew, "Classical Antiquity and the Proslavery Argument," *Slavery and Abolition*, May, 1989.

Hartwell, R.M., *The Industrial Revolution and Economic Growth*.

Hay, Douglas, *Albion's Fatal Tree: Crime and Society in 18th Century England*.

Himmelfarb, Gertrude, *The Idea of Poverty: England in the Early Industrial Age*.

Hellie, Richard, *Slavery in Russia, 1450-1725*.

Hening, William, (editor), *Statutes at Large; Being a Collection of All the Laws of Virginia from the First Session of the Legislature in the Year 1619*.

Herrick, Cheesman A., *White Servitude in Pennsylvania*.

Hilton, Rodney H., "Freedom and Villeinage in England," *Past and Present*, July, 1965.

Hirst, J.B., *Convict Society and Its Enemies*.

Hoffman, Ronald, "The Disaffected in the Revolutionary South," in *The American Revolution: Explorations in the History of American Radicalism*.

Hofstadter, Richard, *Social Darwinism in American Thought*.

Holland, Ruth, *Mill Child*.

Hollis, Patricia, "Anti-Slavery and British Working-Class Radicalism," in *Anti-Slavery, Religion and Reform*.

Homer, Leonard, *On the Employment of Children in Factories*.

Hughes, Robert, *The Fatal Shore*

Hummel, Jeffrey Rogers, "The Civil War," *The United States at War Audio Cassette Series*.

Hurd, J.C., *The Law of Freedom and Bondage in the United States*.

Hyams, Paul, *Kings, Lords and Peasants in Medieval England: The Common Law of Villeinage in the 12th and 13th Centuries*.

Inglis, Brian, *Poverty and the Industrial Revolution*.

Innes, Stephen, *Work and Labor in Early America*.

Jernegan, Marcus W., *Laboring and Dependent Classes in America, 1607-1783*.

Jervey, Theo, "The White Indentured Servants of South Carolina," *South Carolina Historical and Genealogical Magazine, 1911*.

Johnson, Robert C., "The Transportation of Vagrant Children from London to Virginia," in *Early Stuart Studies*.

Jones, Alice H., *Wealth of a Nation to Be: The American Colonies on the Eve of the Revolution. Journals of the Commons House of Assembly of the Province of South Carolina: 1692-1775. Journals of the House of Commons, 1547-1900*.

Kaminkov, Marion and Jack, ed., *Original Lists of Emigrants Bondage from London to the American Colonies, 1719-1744*.

Karras, Ruth Mazo, *Slavery and Society in Medieval Scandinavia*.

Kay, James P., *The Moral and Physical Condition of the Working Classes*.

Kingsbury, Susan, M., (ed.), *The Records of the Virginia Company of London*.

Laurens, Henry, *Laurens' Letters, 1767-1771*.

Lefroy, John H., *Memorials of the Discovery and Early Settlement of the Bermudas or Somers Islands, 1518-1685*.

Lester, Charles Edwards, *The Glory and the Shame of England*.

Levine, Bruce, (et al.), *Who Built America? Working People and the Nation's Economy, Politics, Culture and Society. Vol. I: From Conquest and Colonization Through Reconstruction and the Great Uprising of 1877*.

Ligon, Richard, *A True and Exact History of the Island of Barbados*.
Lucas manuscript, *Bridgetown Public Library, Barbados*.
Mackeson, John F., *Bristol Transported*.
MacLeod, Duncan, *Slavery, Race and the American Revolution*.
MacNiocaill, Geroid, *Ireland Before the Vikings*.
Maithus, T.R., *An Essay on the Principle of Population*.
Mantoux, Paul, *The Industrial Revolution in the 18th Century*.
Markham, Edwin and Lindsey, Benjamin B., and Creel, George, *Children in Bondage*.
McCormac, E.l., *White Servitude in Maryland, 1634-1820*.
McFeely, William S., *Frederic Douglass*.
McKee, Samuel, *Labor in Colonial New York, 1664-1776*.
McIllwaine, H.R., *Journals of the House of Burgesses of Virginia, 1619-1776*.
Melville, Herman, *Redburn: His First Voyage*.
Melville, Herman, *White Jacket*.
Mendelsohn, Isaac, *Slavery in the Ancient Near East*.
Moran, Patrick F., *Historical Sketch of the Persecutions Suffered by the Catholics of Ireland*.
Morgan, Edmund S., *American Slavery, American Freedom*.
Morris, Richard B., *Government and Labor in Early America*
Morris, Richard B., *"Massachusetts and the Common Law," American History Review, 1926*. Nardinelli, Clark, *Child Labor and the Industrial Revolution*.
Neal, Daniel, *The Laws of New England to the Year 1700*.
Norton, Caroline, *"A Voice from the Factories," in The Laboring Classes of England*.
Novack, George, *America's Revolutionary Heritage*.
Nugent, Nell Marion, *Cavaliers and Pioneers: Abstracts of Virginia Land Patents and Grants, 1623-1666*.
O'Brien, Bronterre, *The Rise, Progress and Phases of Human Slavery*.
Oldmixon, John, *The British Empire in America*.

Pelteret, David A.E., *Late Anglo-Saxon Slavery. (Canadian Theses on Microfiche).*

Perkins, Edwin J., *The Economy of Colonial America.*

Philips, Ulrich B., *Life and Labor in the Old South.*

Phillips, George L., *England's Climbing-Boys.*

Phillips, William D., *Slavery from Roman Times to the Early Transatlantic Trade.*

Prebble, John, *Glencoe.*

Prebble, John, *The Highland Clearances.*

Probate Court Records 1672-1779. Charleston, South Carolina.

Quimby, Ian, *Apprenticeship in Colonial Philadelphia.*

Rayback, Joseph G., *A History of American Labor.*

Register for the Privy Council of Scotland.

Rediker, Marcus, *Between the Devil and the Deep Blue Sea.*

Reid, Richard, "A Test Case of the 'Crying Evil': Desertion Among North Carolina Troops During the Civil War," *North Carolina Historical Review, Summer, 1981.*

Richardson, Samuel, *The Apprentice's Vade Mecum.*

Riley, Edward M., ed., *The Journal of John Harrower: An Indentured Servant in the Colony of Virginia, 1773-1776.*

Rivers, Marcellus and Foyle, Oxenbridge, *England's Slaves or Barbados' Merchandise.*

Roediger, David R., *The Wages of Whiteness: Race and the Making of the American Working Class.*

Rose, Willie Lee, *A Documentary History of Slavery in North America.*

Ruchames, L., "Sources of Racial Thought in Colonial America," *Journal of Negro History, number 52.*

Russell, John Henderson, *Free Negro in Virginia 1619-1865.*

Salinger, Sharon V., *To Serve Well and Faithfully: Labor and Indentured Servants in Pennsylvania, 1682-1800.*

Schweninger, Loren, *Black Property Owners in the South: 1790-1915.*

Seybolt, Robert F., *Apprenticeship and Apprenticeship Education in Colonial New England and New York.*

Shaw, A.G.L., *Convicts and the Colonies.*
Shaw, Charles, *When I Was a Child.*
Sheppard, Jill, *The 'Redlegs' of Barbados: Their Origins and History.*
Siebert, W.H., *"Slavery and Servitude in East Florida, 1726-1776," Quarterly Periodical of the Florida Historical Society, July, 1931.*
Smith, Abbot Emerson, *Colonists in Bondage.*
Smith, Billy G., *The 'Lower Sort': Philadelphia's Laboring People, 1750-1800.*
Smith, Warren B., *White Servitude in Colonial South Carolina.*
Stowe, Harriet Beecher, *Sunny Memories.*
Stowe manuscript, (324), British Museum.
Ste. Croix, G.E.M. de, *Slavery and Other Forms of Unfree Labor.*
Taylor, William, *The White Slave's Complaint.*
Thompson, E. P., *The Making of the English Working Class.*
Thomson, William, *A Tradesman's Travels.*
Thornbrough, Emma Lou, "The Race Issue in Indiana Politics During the Civil War," *Indiana Magazine of History, June, 1951.*
Tomlins, Christopher, "The Ties that Bind: Master and Servant in Massachusetts, 1800-1850," *Labor History, Spring, 1989.*
Tragicall Relation of the Virginia Assembly. Library of Congress.
Tree, Ronald, *A History of Barbados.*
Trefousse, Hans L., *Andrew Johnson: A Biography.*
Trollope, Frances, *Domestic Manners.*
Trollope, Frances, *The Life and Adventures of Michael Armstrong, Factory Boy.*
Uchteritz, Heinrich von, *Kurze Reise.*
Van Der Lee, John, *Bound Over: Indentured Servitude and the American Conscience.*
Verlinden, Charles, *The Slave in Medieval Europe.*
Wakefield, Edward Gibbon, *England and America: A Comparison of the Social and Political State of Both Nations.*
Ward, Harry M., *Colonial America: 1607-1763.*
Ward, J.T., *The Factory Movement: 1830-1855.*

Watson, Alan, *Slave Law in the Americas*.

Wergeland, Agnes Mathilde, *Slavery in Germanic Society During the Middle Ages*.

Werner, John M., *Reaping the Bloody Harvest*.

Whistler, Henry, *Journal of the West India Expedition*.

White, Pliny H., *Life and Services of Matthew Lyon*.

Wiedemann, Thomas, *Greek and Roman Slavery*.

Williams, Carl O., *Thralldom in Ancient Iceland*.

Williams, Eric, *Capitalism and Slavery*.

Williams, Eric, *From Columbus to Castro: The History of the Caribbean*.

Williamson, Peter, *The Life and Curious Adventures of Peter Williamson, Who Was Carried Off From Aberdeen and Sold for a Slave*.

Williamson, Peter, *State of the Process, Peter Williamson Against William Fordyce and Others*. British Museum.

Willis, Arthur J., *A Calendar of South Hampton Apprenticeship Registers*.

Wood, Michael, *In Search of the Dark Ages*.

Young, Brian, *The Villein's Bible*.

OTHER BOOKS BY THE AUTHOR

Cryptocurrency Millionaire Make Money With Cryptocurrency

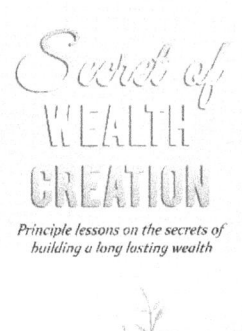

Secret Of Wealth Creation: Principle Lessons On The Secrets Of Building A Long Lasting Wealth

Guide To Private Placement Project Fundingtrade Programs: Understanding High-Level Project Funding Trade Programs

Make Money Doing Nothing

The Blueprint To Intelligent Investors

The Blueprint To Intelligent Investors Volume 2

Financial Intelligence: Fundamentals Of Private Placement Programs (PPP)

Private Placement Programs - The Holy Grail

Special Drawing Rights (SDR) And The Federal Reserve

Special Drawing Rights (SDR) And The Federal Reserve Volume 2.

Cryptocurrency: The Next Level For Banking Reform

Fundamentals Of Buy/Sell Investment Trading Programs

Sir Patrick Bijou

INDUSTRY OVERVIEW

JOURNAL

SIR PATRICK BIJOU

Unsurpassed Relationships in Wealth Management

www.ingramcontent.com/pod-product-compliance
Lightning Source LLC
Chambersburg PA
CBHW061230070526
44584CB00030B/4067